The American Cookbook

The AMERICAN COOKBOOK

Recipes made in the USA

★★★ Contents

Foreword

When you think about it, there's no such thing as any one particular direction in American cuisine. The USA is the original country of immigration – which has, of course, left its culinary tracks. As the waves of immigrants from various countries and nationalities arrived, they all brought recipes from their old homes with them to the land of unlimited opportunities. Over the course of time, the recipes gradually altered, blending with foreign recipes, and continued to develop. But depending on where and when a majority of the various settlers made their new homes, the culinary preferences of the original homelands are still evident in the cuisine of today. Of course, the geographical features of the different areas also determine their regional kitchen practices. Large lakes and rivers provide a variety of freshwater fish; vast cattle ranches in the interior of the land ensure that there is a wide range of meat dishes, and unspoilt forests and mountains provide game for the menus.

REGIONAL FEATURES

• Great Plains and Rocky Mountains - the states of North Dakota, South Dakota, Nebraska, Kansas, Oklahoma, Montana, Wyoming, Colorado, Utah, Idaho, and Nevada

Today, America's "granaries" are also home to countless cattle ranches. That's why juicy steaks are particularly popular in this plain, down-to-earth cuisine. As we move further north towards the Rocky Mountains, game and salmon are naturally included in the typical regional specialities.

• New England - the states of Maine, New Hampshire, Vermont, Massachusetts, Connecticut and Rhode Island

The extremely varied cuisine of this region impresses in particular with its fish recipes and desserts. The first settlers were the Puritans from England, and they adopted the forms of preparation used by the Native Americans for the region's typical vegetables such as pumpkin and corn. This developed into a unique combination. Whether pumpkin pie or apple pie, many of the baked and sweet specialities that are so popular all over America originated in New England. And Thanksgiving, with its typical meal of turkey, also has its roots in this relatively small geographic area.

• The mid-Atlantic coast - the states of New York, New Jersey, Maryland, Pennsylvania, Delaware, and the District of Columbia

Dutch, Scandinavians, Italians, Chinese, Germans and English – they all left their culinary footprints here. To say nothing of the exiting metropolitan cuisine of New York City, down-to-earth rural food and geographically both the coast with its abundance of seafood and fish, and the interior of the land with its typical poultry and vegetable dishes: the cuisine of the mid-Atlantic coast is the most diverse in the entire country. For this book, we have mainly chosen New York specialities such as eggs Benedict, Caesar's salad and French toast.

• The Southern States - Virginia, West Virginia, Kentucky, Tennessee, Arkansas, North Carolina, South Carolina, Georgia, Mississippi, Alabama, Louisiana and Florida

There is much evidence of African and Indian influences here. Spicy dishes such as gumbos, and ingredients such as black

beans, are typical of the Southern States — and are, of course, also included in this collection of recipes. As is the region's best-known dessert: its legendary pecan pie, a really rich tart with lots of pecan nuts. Louisiana's cuisine holds a very special position. With French, Spanish and Caribbean-Cuban influences, it is an extremely exciting, multi-cultural, unique cuisine that is currently the target of much interest. Cajuns, jambalayas and exotically, clever compositions of prawns, chicken and fruit with hot spices have their fans the world over — and their numbers are increasing. Don't be nervous: take the opportunity to try the unusual compositions — we know you will be delighted with them!

• The South West - the states of Texas, Arizona and New Mexico

This region of cowboys and vast cattle ranches is known for its tradition of BBQs, juicy steaks and the many different bean and rice dishes, the recipes which were originally adopted from the Native Americans. It is also home to the decidedly popular Tex-Mex dishes such as enchiladas, tortillas, guacamole and so on, the tastiest examples of which are also to be found between the covers of this book.

• The Pacific Coast states - California, Washington, Oregon, Alaska and Hawaii

Of course, there is an abundance of fish on menus everywhere, but in all other respects the cuisines of the various states differ tremendously. After all, there are about 4000 km between Alaska and California, as the crow flies. Whereas the cuisine of Washington, Oregon, and Alaska is generally plain and down-to-earth, that of California loves to experiment, and delights with light, fresh, healthy cross-over recipes with European, Asian and Central American influences. Even in its hearty dishes, Hawaiian cuisine often uses pineapple, coconut, and macadamia nuts — an exotic combination that packs quite a punch.

• Midwest - the states of Ohio, Michigan, Indiana, Illinois, Wisconsin, Minnesota, Iowa and Missouri

As you would expect, the regional vast lakes contain an abundance of freshwater fish such as trout and pike that are also found on its menus. And all are prepared in the most diverse ways. The cuisine tends to be quite plain and rustic, evidence of the Dutch and Scandinavian roots of the first settlers, and also contains numerous hearty meat dishes.

NATIONAL COMMONALITIES

American classics from all over the States are to be found in its diners. Originally intended to provide hungry factory workers with good food, they have over time become a typical American institution. Blueberry pancakes for breakfast, meat loaf, hamburgers or tuna noodle casserole for lunch, New York cheesecake to finish with: diner dishes are loved and popular all over America — and also to be found in this book, of course. However, despite all the regional differences, all in all, the American cuisine is one that is hearty, filling, and — above all — makes you feel good. Perhaps that's the reason why it's so popular!

We hope you enjoy cooking the recipes in this book — and eating the end results even more so!

Salads, appetisers and soups

Whether Caesar's salad, a BLT sandwich or pumpkin soup — popular classic appetisers and soups are found all over the USA.

French toast with dip

Serves 4

PREPARATION TIME: approx. 20 minutes (plus cooking time)

To make the toasts, first whisk the eggs and milk in a bowl. Season with salt, pepper and a little paprika. Heat the maize germ oil and butter in two pans.

Dip the bread in the egg and milk until they have absorbed it well but are not at the point of disintegrating. Put 1 slice each of ham and cheese on 4 slices of bread, and top with the other 4 slices of bread. Put 2 double toasts in a pan and fry over a medium heat for about 12 minutes until golden, turning once.

To make the dip, finely chop the gherkins. Wash and shake dry the tarragon and finely chop the leaves. Combine both in a bowl with mustard, ketchup, gherkin liquid and olive oil, and season to taste with salt and pepper.

Cut the toasts in half diagonally, and arrange on plates with the gherkin dip. Garnish with tomato slices and serve.

FOR THE TOAST
4 eggs
250 ml milk
salt
pepper
pinch of paprika powder
2 tbsp maize germ oil
20 g butter
8 slices bread for toasting
4 thin slices cooked ham
4 slices young Gouda

FOR THE DIP
100 g pickled gherkins
3 tarragon stalks
1 tbsp coarse-grained sweet mustard
1 tbsp ketchup
7 tbsp gherkin brine
3 tbsp olive oil
salt
pepper

ADDITIONALLY
tomato slices to garnish

NUTRITION INFORMATION: 430 kcal ‖ 1790 kJ ‖ 20 g protein ‖ 32 g fat ‖ 15 g carbohydrate

Eggs Benedict on toast

Serves 4

FOR THE HOLLANDAISE SAUCE
150 g butter
3 egg yolks
½ tsp mustard
salt
1 tsp lemon juice
dash of Tabasco

FOR THE TOAST
8 bacon slices
5 tbsp white wine vinegar
salt
4 eggs
4 slices bread for toasting

PREPARATION TIME: approx. 35 minutes

First make the hollandaise sauce. Cut the butter into pieces and melt in a pan. Remove from the hob.

Whisk together the egg yolks, mustard, a little salt, lemon juice and Tabasco in a stick blender. Then add the melted butter, first in drops and then in a thin stream. Keep blending it as you do so.

Keep the sauce warm in a bowl over a hot bain-marie, stirring it from time to time. Make sure it does not get too warm, as otherwise it will separate.

To make the toast, first fry the bacon in a pan without oil until crispy. Set aside. Bring about 1.5 litres of water to the boil, and flavour with white wine vinegar and a little salt. Reduce the heat so the water is just gently simmering.

Carefully break the eggs individually into a metal ladle. Hold in the simmering water until the eggs have just set on the outside. Then let the eggs glide off the ladle, and poach for about 4 minutes.

Toast the bread. Place 2 slices of bacon on 1 slice of toast and put 1 egg on top. Serve with a little of the hollandaise sauce.

NUTRITION INFORMATION: 530 kcal | 2200 kJ | 12 g protein | 49 g fat | 11 g carbohydrate

California wrap

Serves 4

PREPARATION TIME: approx. 30 minutes

Pre-heat the oven to 180 °C (Gas Mark 4). Wash and pick over the spinach, then spin dry and shred the leaves if necessary. Wash and spin dry the coriander and pluck off the leaves. Peel and thinly slice the onion. Wash, dry, trim and thinly slice the spring onion. Combine in a bowl.

Devein the shrimps and rinse under running cold water. Pat dry and season with salt and pepper. Heat the oil and fry the shrimps for about 8 minutes until done. Shred the smoked salmon. Peel the avocados. Remove the stones and slice the flesh. Immediately combine with the lemon juice.

Heat the tortillas in the oven for about 5 minutes. Remove, then open out and spread with the cream cheese to just before the edges.

Arrange the smoked salmon on top. Sprinkle with the spinach, coriander and onion mixture. Arrange the shrimps on the filling. Pat the avocados dry with paper towels and arrange over the filling. Finish by drizzling 1 tablespoon of chilli sauce over each wrap. Roll up the wraps. Cut in half diagonally if desired, and secure with wooden sticks. Serve the California wraps immediately.

50 g baby leaf spinach
½ bunch coriander
1 red onion
1 spring onion
150 g shrimps (ready to use)
salt
pepper
2 tbsp oil
200 g smoked salmon
2 ripe avocados
2 tbsp lemon juice
4 tortillas
120 g cream cheese
4 tbsp sweet chilli sauce

NUTRITION INFORMATION: 530 kcal ǀ 2240 kJ ǀ 20 g protein ǀ 37 g fat ǀ 30 g carbohydrate

Cobb salad

Serves 4

FOR THE SALAD

2 eggs
1 romaine lettuce
1 radicchio
4 plum tomatoes
2 bunches chives
150 g mild blue cheese
1 avocado
2 tbsp lemon juice
8 bacon slices
4 chicken breasts
salt
pepper
paprika powder

FOR THE DRESSING

3 tbsp sunflower oil
3 tbsp olive oil
2 ½ tbsp red wine vinegar
3 tbsp orange juice
1 tbsp Dijon mustard
salt
pepper
pinch of sugar

PREPARATION TIME: approx. 40 minutes

Pierce the eggs and boil for about 8 minutes until hard. Rinse under cold water, then peel and leave to cool. Trim, wash and spin dry the romaine lettuce and radicchio, and tear into bite-size pieces. Wash and pat dry the tomatoes, then cut out the stalks and cut the flesh into strips. Wash and pat dry the chives and cut into thin rings. Crumble the blue cheese with your fingers. Peel the avocados. Remove the stones and thinly slice the flesh. Sprinkle with lemon juice.

Fry the bacon in a pan without oil until crisp. Wash and pat dry the chicken breasts and cut in half lengthways. Season with salt, pepper and a little paprika, and fry in the bacon fat for about 10 minutes until done. Turn only once so that a nice golden crust develops on the chicken. Remove from the pan and leave to cool. Slice the hard boiled eggs.

Arrange the salad leaves on four plates with the sliced tomatoes and eggs on top. Pat dry the avocado slices and place over the salad, and finish by crumbling the blue cheese on top. Cut the chicken breasts into bite-size pieces and arrange on the salad like roof tiles; likewise the bacon slices. Sprinkle over the chive rolls.

Whisk together the two oils, vinegar, orange juice and mustard for the dressing. Season well with salt and pepper, and finish with a little sugar. Drizzle teaspoons of the dressing over the salad.

Tip: You can vary this salad in almost any way you like. For instance, you can also add sweetcorn, or use onion rings or cress instead of the chives.

NUTRITION INFORMATION: 670 kcal | 2800 kJ | 45 g protein | 51 g fat | 6 g carbohydrate

Caesar's salad

Serves 4

PREPARATION TIME: approx. 40 minutes

Trim, wash and spin dry the lettuce hearts, and tear into bite-size pieces. Put in a bowl.

Cut the bacon into strips, and fry in a pan without oil until crisp. Remove, then place on paper towels and set aside. Cut the crusts off the bread, and dice the bread into cubes about 0.5 cm square. Heat the butter and sunflower oil in a pan and fry the bread on all sides until crisp. Place on paper towels to drain, and again set aside.

To make the dressing, pierce the egg and cook in boiling water for 2 minutes. Separate the egg white and yolk. Put the egg yolk in a tall container. Rinse and pat dry the anchovies. Peel and finely chop the garlic clove. Blend both together with the lemon juice, mustard and Worcester sauce. Then slowly add the olive oil in a thin stream, stirring in well. Season the dressing with salt and pepper.

Pour the dressing over the salad and combine well. Arrange the salad on plates. Sprinkle over the bacon and croutons. Grate the Parmesan over the top, and serve immediately.

FOR THE SALAD
4 romaine lettuce hearts
100 g bacon
4 slices bread for toasting
2 tbsp butter
1 tbsp sunflower oil

FOR THE DRESSING
1 egg
3 anchovies
1 garlic clove
4 tbsp lemon juice
1 tbsp mustard
1 tsp Worcester sauce
100 ml olive oil
salt
pepper

ADDITIONALLY
100 g Parmesan

Black bean soup

Serves 4

PREPARATION TIME: approx. 30 minutes (plus soaking and cooking time)

Cover the beans with plenty of cold water and leave to soak overnight. Next day, drain in a sieve, then rinse and leave.

Chop the bacon into small cubes. Chop the ham. Peel and finely chop the onion and garlic cloves. Trim, peel and finely chop the carrot.

Heat the olive oil in a large saucepan. Fry the ham and bacon over a medium heat for 10 minutes, stirring continuously. Add the onion and carrot. Cook for a further 3 minutes. Then add the chopped garlic and stir in. Now add the beans, beef bouillon and 1 litre of water. Add the bay leaf, crumble in the chilli and stir in the cumin and oregano to season. Stir well and bring to the boil, then simmer gently over a low heat for 1 hour 30 minutes until the beans are soft.

Scoop out about half of the beans and a little liquid and blend to a paste in a stick blender. Put this paste back in the saucepan, and combine with the whole beans. Season the soup with vinegar, sherry, salt and pepper, and simmer for a further 30 minutes.

To serve, combine the soured cream and lemon juice, and season with salt and pepper. Ladle the soup into bowls and top with a dollop of soured cream to serve.

250 g dried black beans
50 g bacon
50 g smoked ham
1 onion
2 garlic cloves
1 carrot
2 tbsp olive oil
1 l beef bouillon
1 bay leaf
1 dried chilli pepper
1 tsp ground cumin seed
1 tsp dried oregano
1 tbsp red wine vinegar
1 tbsp sherry
salt
pepper
200 g light soured cream
1 tbsp lemon juice

Serves 4

6 iceberg lettuce leaves
3 tomatoes
16 slices of bacon
8 slices bread for toasting
4 tbsp mayonnaise
1 tbsp mustard
salt
pepper

Bacon, lettuce and tomato sandwich

PREPARATION TIME: approx. 20 minutes

Wash and spin dry the iceberg lettuce, and break into small pieces. Wash, dry, trim and slice the tomatoes. Fry the bacon in a pan without oil, then place on paper towels to drain. Toast the bread.

Combine the mayonnaise and mustard. Spread the mustard mayonnaise on the toast. Arrange the iceberg lettuce on all 8 slices, along with the tomatoes. Season with salt and pepper, but not too much as the bacon will be salty. Arrange the bacon on 4 slices of the toast. Fold or trim it so that it does not go over the sides of the bread.

Top with the toast without the bacon, holding the filling with your hands. Press down lightly on the sandwiches, then cut in half diagonally. Arrange on plates and serve immediately.

NUTRITION INFORMATION: 340 kcal | 1400 kJ | 7 g protein | 23 g fat | 24 g carbohydrate

Pumpkin soup

Serves 4

1 small muscat pumpkin
1 tbsp olive oil
1 onion
2 garlic cloves
50 g butter
2 tsp brown sugar
½ tsp salt and pepper
big pinch each of cinnamon, mace and nutmeg
500 ml milk
750 ml chicken bouillon
a little lemon juice
100 ml cream
few drops of pumpkin seed oil

PREPARATION TIME: approx. 30 minutes (plus baking, cooling and cooking time)

Pre-heat the oven to 180 °C (Gas Mark 4). Wash the pumpkin and cut in half. Scoop out the seeds and fibres. Cut 1 kg of the flesh into slices and arrange on a baking tray. Brush lightly with olive oil and roast in the oven for about 45 minutes. Remove from the oven and leave to cool. Peel.

Meanwhile, peel and finely chop the onion and garlic cloves. Melt the butter in a saucepan and sauté the onion and garlic for about 10 minutes. Add the pumpkin flesh and sprinkle over the sugar. Add the salt, pepper and other spices and simmer for a further 10 minutes or so, stirring continuously. Then pour over the milk and chicken bouillon and bring to the boil, stirring all the time.

Remove the saucepan from the heat and blend until smooth. Season with a little lemon juice. Whip the cream and stir in a few drops of pumpkin seed oil. Ladle the soup into bowls. Stir in a dollop of cream to finish, and serve immediately.

NUTRITION INFORMATION: 350 kcal | 1470 kJ | 8 g protein | 26 g fat | 22 g carbohydrate

Hushpuppies

Serves 4 - makes approx. 12

50 g sweetcorn (fresh, frozen or canned)
125 g polenta
75 g flour
1 tsp baking powder
½ tsp baking soda
50 g cheddar
2 spring onions
salt
pepper
paprika powder
1 egg
125 ml buttermilk
approx. 500 ml oil for deep-frying

PREPARATION TIME: approx. 30 minutes

Wash and pat dry the fresh sweetcorn. Allow the frozen sweetcorn to defrost. Rinse and drain canned sweetcorn in a sieve. Stir together the polenta, flour, baking powder and baking soda in a bowl.

Grate the cheddar. Wash, dry and trim the spring onions, then thinly slice the white and light green parts. Add both to the polenta mixture, and season with salt, pepper and paprika powder.

Whisk together the egg and buttermilk, and stir into the polenta mixture. Add the sweetcorn. Only stir long enough to combine the ingredients.

Heat the oil. If you hold the handle of a wooden spoon in it and it starts to bubble, then the oil should be hot enough at about 180 °C. Now scoop out balls of the dough and shape into balls with two tablespoons. Fry in the hot oil for about 3 minutes until golden. Lift out with a slotted spoon, and place on paper towels for a few moments to drain. Dust with salt and paprika powder, and serve while still hot.

NUTRITION INFORMATION: 440 kcal | 1860 kJ | 11 g protein | 27 g fat | 40 g carbohydrate

Meat and poultry dishes

Burgers, tasty pies, juicy steaks and hearty casseroles – the Southern States and former "Wild West" show how basic ingredients can be turned into delicious, down-to-earth meals.

Arroz con pollo

Serves 4

1 large chicken
400 g chorizo
2 onions
2 garlic cloves
1 green pepper
1 green chilli pepper
2 beef tomatoes
½ bunch thyme
1 tbsp maize germ oil
pinch of sugar
175 g long-grain rice
150 g sweetcorn (fresh, frozen or canned)
500 ml chicken bouillon
75 g mild red peppers in oil
1 bunch coriander
salt
pepper

PREPARATION TIME: approx. 50 minutes (plus cooking time)

Pre-heat the oven to 180 °C (Gas Mark 4). Wash the chicken inside and out and pat dry. Divide into 8 pieces. Cut the chorizo into slices about 0.5 cm thick. Peel and chop the onions and garlic cloves. Halve and trim the peppers, then wash on the inside and out and pat dry. Cut the pepper into strips and chop the chilli. Wash, dry, trim and deseed the tomatoes, and finely chop the flesh. Wash and pat dry the thyme and pluck off the leaves.

Heat a large casserole dish. Put the chorizo slices in the casserole, then cook over a low heat for about 15 minutes until the fat runs and the sausage is crisp. Lift out and set aside. Pour away all but 1 tablespoon of the cooking oil. Add the maize germ oil and heat. Fry the chicken pieces in portions over a high heat on all sides for about 8 minutes. Remove. Lower the heat again.

Now sauté the onions in the remainder of the cooking oil, and add the garlic, sliced pepper and chopped chilli. Cook briefly, then stir in the tomatoes. Stir in the sugar and thyme, then the rice and sweetcorn. (If using canned sweetcorn, rinse and drain first. Defrost frozen sweetcorn.) Pour over the bouillon and bring to the boil. Dice and stir in the peppers in oil. Arrange the sausage and chicken over this mixture, and cover with a lid. Put the casserole in the oven and bake for about 35 minutes.

Then remove the lid and increase the oven temperature to 200 °C (Gas Mark 6). Leave the rice in the oven for a further 10 minutes. Wash and spin dry the coriander and pluck off the leaves. Season the rice casserole with salt and pepper, and sprinkle with the coriander to serve.

NUTRITION INFORMATION: 1180 kcal | 4950 kJ | 97 g protein | 68 g fat | 44 g carbohydrate

Grilled porterhouse steak
with salsa

PREPARATION TIME: approx. 30 minutes (plus standing and cooking time)

Cut the fat rind on the steak back to about 0.7 cm. Slit the remaining fat several times with a knife, taking care not to cut into the meat. This will prevent the meat from curling during cooking, and helps it to cook evenly. Peel and halve the garlic clove, and rub the meat with the cut surfaces. Drizzle the olive oil over the meat and season well with pepper. Massage the oil and pepper onto both sides of the meat using your hands. Wrap in clingfilm and leave at room temperature for about 1 hour.

Meanwhile, heat the grill and prepare the salsa: Wash, dry and trim the spring onions, and very thinly slice the white and light green parts. Halve and trim the peppers, then wash on the inside and out and pat dry. Finely dice the pepper and chop the chillies. Wash and spin dry the coriander and mint and pluck off the leaves. Peel and chop the garlic cloves. Then finely chop the herb leaves, and combine in a bowl with the spring onions, pepper, chilli and garlic.

Wash, pat dry, trim and deseed the tomatoes. Finely chop the flesh. Squeeze the limes. Add the juice and diced tomatoes to the other ingredients for the salsa. Stir well, and season with salt, pepper and a little cumin. Cover and chill until required.

Brush the BBQ rack with oil, and put in a fairly low position over the coals. Salt the steak and grill over a high heat for 1 minute on each side. Then raise the rack, and cook each side of the meat for a further 10 minutes or so. It should still be pink on the inside. Remove from the BBQ and wrap in aluminium foil. Leave to rest for about 5 minutes. Cut the meat off the bone, and cut into slices, working diagonally to the fibres. Serve with the salsa and crispy bread, or with fries and BBQ sauce.

Tip: Perfect preparation without a BBQ: first flash-fry the meat in a grill pan for about 2 minutes on each side, then finish in the Pre-heated oven at 130 °C (Gas Mark 0.5) for about 50 minutes. Preferybly usc a meat thermometer to measure the core temperature. It should be 57–58 °C.

Serves 4

FOR THE STEAK
1 porterhouse steak (approx. 5 cm thick, 1.5 kg, order in advance from your butcher)
1 garlic clove
3 tbsp olive oil
pepper
salt

FOR THE SALSA
4 spring onions
1 green pepper
2 green chilli peppers
1 bunch coriander
1 bunch mint
2 garlic cloves
2 tomatoes
2 limes
salt
pepper
cumin seeds

ADDITIONALLY
oil for the rack

NUTRITION INFORMATION: 540 kcal | 2260 kJ | 75 g protein | 23 g fat | 6 g carbohydrate

Giant burger

Serves 4

FOR THE BURGER SAUCE
3 tbsp BBQ sauce
3 tbsp ketchup
3 tbsp mayonnaise
1 tsp mustard
1 tsp balsamic vinegar
dash of Worcester sauce
salt
pepper
pinch of sugar

FOR THE BURGERS
4 lettuce or lollo rosso leaves
2 tomatoes
4 pickled gherkins
1 white onion
1 red onion
1 kg minced beef
2 tsp mustard
1 tsp Worcester sauce
1 tsp salt
1 tsp pepper
3 tbsp sunflower oil
8 slices of bacon
8 slices processed cheese
4 hamburger buns

PREPARATION TIME: approx. 30 minutes

First make the burger sauce. Combine the BBQ sauce, ketchup, mayonnaise, mustard, balsamic vinegar and Worcester sauce. Season well with salt and pepper, and finish with a little sugar.

Trim, wash and spin dry the lettuce leaves. Wash and pat dry the tomatoes, then cut out the stalks and cut the flesh into thin strips. Cut the gherkins lengthwise into thin slices. Peel and finely chop the white onion. Peel and thinly slice the red onion. Pre-heat the grill of the oven.

Put the minced beef, chopped onion, mustard, Worcester sauce, salt and pepper in a bowl, combine well. Shape into 8 flat burgers of about the same diameter as the buns.

Heat the oil in a pan and flash-fry the burgers on both sides over a high heat to make a nice crust, then lower the heat and cook for about 10 minutes on each side. In a second pan, fry the bacon without oil until crisp. Just before the end of the cooking time, put 1 slice of cheese on each burger and continue cooking until the cheese starts to melt. Meanwhile, cut open the buns and place the cut side down on the oven grill to toast.

Now assemble the burgers: put the lettuce on the bottom halves. On top of that – 1 burger, and on top of that 1 tablespoon of burger sauce. Then arrange the tomato slices and bacon on top. Put the second burger on the tomato and bacon, and cover it with the gherkins, red onion rings and the remainder of the burger sauce. Place the top half of the buns on top, and serve immediately.

NUTRITION INFORMATION: 910 kcal | 3810 kJ | 61 g protein | 61 g fat | 30 g carbohydrate

Chicken pot pie

PREPARATION TIME: approx. 1 hour 30 minutes (plus cooking, cooling and baking time)

To make the pastry, sift the flour into a bowl. Add the butter, cut into small pieces, and the cream cheese. Knead well with a good pinch of salt and the vinegar to make a smooth dough. Work out on a floured worktop to the size of the dish that you will be using for the pie. Wrap in aluminium foil and chill for about 1 hour.

Wash the chicken. Put in a saucepan and cover with water. Peel and quarter the onion. Trim, peel and quarter the carrots. Wash, trim and chop 1 leek and the celery. Add to the chicken with a little salt, the clove and the pimento seeds, and simmer over a low heat for about 50 minutes. Then drain in a sieve, reserving the cooking liquid. Leave the chicken to cool, then remove the skin. Strip the flesh off the bones and cut into bite-size pieces. Trim and wash the second leak, and cut the white and pale green piece into rings. Defrost the peas.

Pre-heat the oven to 200 °C (Gas Mark 6). Trim the mushrooms and wipe with damp kitchen paper. Peel the potato and chop into small dice. Heat the oil in a saucepan and fry the mushrooms all over, allowing them to colour slightly. Lift out with a slotted spoon. Now add the leek, potato and peas. Sauté briefly, then pour over 400 ml of the chicken bouillon and simmer, uncovered, for about 7 minutes. Lift out the vegetables and set aside.

Melt the butter in a casserole dish. Dust over the flour and cook for about 2 minutes. Pour over 250 ml of the cooking liquid and bring to the boil, stirring continuously. Stir in the cream, milk, salt, pepper, nutmeg and herbs. Return to the boil, then stir in the drained vegetables, chicken and mushrooms. Allow the pastry to warm up slightly, then place over the dish and press the sides down well. Brush with milk and pierce several times with a knife to allow the steam to escape. Bake in the oven for about 25 minutes until golden.

Serves 4

FOR THE PASTRY
180 g flour
125 g cold butter
125 g cream cheese
salt
1 tbsp white wine vinegar

FOR THE FILLING
1 chicken (approx. 1.8 kg)
1 onion
2 carrots
2 leeks
1 celery stalk
salt
1 clove
5 pimento seeds
125 g frozen peas
150 g young button mushrooms
1 waxy potato
1 tbsp oil
40 g butter
30 g flour
125 ml cream
125 ml milk
pepper
nutmeg
3 tbsp freshly chopped mixed herbs

ADDITIONALLY
flour for the worktop
milk to brush

NUTRITION INFORMATION: 1450 kcal | 6240 kJ | 74 g protein | 109 g fat | 55 g carbohydrate

Barbecued spare ribs
with old-fashioned cole slaw

Serves 4

FOR THE SPARE RIBS

1 onion
2 garlic cloves
1 red chilli pepper
2 cm ginger
2 tbsp oil
1 can peeled tomatoes (400 g)
175 ml ketchup
100 ml freshly squeezed orange juice
3 tbsp lemon juice
3 tbsp red wine vinegar
1 tbsp honey
40 g brown sugar
3 tbsp chilli sauce
1 tbsp Worcester sauce
dash of Tabasco
1 tsp mustard
1 tsp ground cumin seed, salt
1.8 kg spare ribs

FOR THE COLE SLAW

3 slices of bacon
800 g cabbage
1 carrot
1 green pepper
1 onion
½ bunch parsley
200 g mayonnaise
100 g light soured cream
1 tbsp mustard
3 tbsp beef bouillon
salt

ADDITIONALLY

oil for the rack

PREPARATION TIME: approx. 50 minutes (plus cooking, marinating and grilling time)

Peel and finely chop the onion and garlic cloves. Halve and trim the chilli pepper, then wash on the inside and out. Pat dry and chop the chilli. Peel and finely grate the ginger. Heat the oil in a saucepan and fry the onion until it just starts to change colour. Then add the garlic, chilli and ginger and sauté for a few minutes. Stir in the peeled tomatoes, ketchup, orange and lemon juice, vinegar, honey, sugar, chilli and Worcester sauces. Add the Tabasco, mustard, cumin seeds and ½ teaspoon of salt. Bring to the boil, stirring, then cover with a lid and simmer over a low heat for about 1 hour. Check the seasoning and leave to cool. Brush half the sauce over the spare ribs and marinate for 3 hours.

Brush a grill rack with oil. Grill the spare ribs under a medium heat for about 40 minutes, turning frequently and brushing with the remainder of the marinade.

To make the cole slaw, first fry the bacon in a pan without oil until the fat runs and the bacon turns crispy. Drain on paper towels and leave until cool, then crumble into small pieces. Set aside.

Trim the cabbage and grate into thin strips. Peel, trim and grate the carrot. Halve and trim the pepper, then wash inside and out, pat dry, and dice finely. Peel and thinly slice the onion. Wash and spin dry the parsley and chop the leaves. Put the vegetables and parsley in a bowl. Combine the mayonnaise, soured cream, mustard and beef bouillon. Season with salt and stir into the salad. Sprinkle over the crumbled bacon. Serve the spare ribs with the cole slaw and white bread.

NUTRITION INFORMATION: 1200 kcal | 5050 kJ | 43 g protein | 98 g fat | 41 g carbohydrate

Roasted chicken
with oranges

Serves 4

PREPARATION TIME: approx. 1 hour (plus cooking time)

Pre-heat the oven to 180 °C (Gas Mark 4). Cut the crusts off the bread and dice the bread into small cubes. Bake in the oven until crispy. Wash, trim and finely dice the celery. Wash and pat dry the herbs and chop the leaves. Peel and finely grate the ginger. Wash the oranges in hot water, dry them and grate the zest of one. Squeeze the juice out of one and cut the other into segments, retaining the juice. Melt the butter in a small saucepan. Combine the bread cubes, celery, half the herbs and the orange segments. Add the butter and knead together with salt, pepper, cumin and a tiny amount of chicken bouillon.

Wash the chickens inside and out and pat dry. Peel and halve the garlic cloves and rub all over the chickens. Season with salt and pepper and stuff with the bread mixture. Secure with wooden sticks and bind with kitchen twine. Put on the drip pan and roast for about 1 hour. Baste occasionally with the cooking juices. The chicken is done if the juices run clear when pierced with a cocktail stick.

To make the sauce, bring the remainder of the chicken bouillon to the boil with the vinegar, sugar, ginger, orange zest and orange juice. Stir in the remainder of the herbs except the parsley. Stir together the cornflour and coconut milk until smooth and pour into the simmering bouillon. Bring to the boil, stirring continuously, until the sauce is nice and thick. Season with salt and pepper.

Remove the chickens from the oven and carve. Stir the roasting juices into the orange sauce. Sprinkle the chicken pieces, stuffing and orange sauce with a little parsley and serve. Rice goes well with this dish.

100 g bread for toasting
2 celery stalks
1 bunch tarragon
1 bunch thyme
2 cm ginger
2 unwaxed oranges
60 g butter
salt
pepper
1 tsp cumin seeds
400 ml chicken bouillon
2 chickens (approx. 1 kg each)
2 garlic cloves
6 tbsp white wine vinegar
3 tbsp brown sugar
1 tbsp cornflour
100 ml coconut milk
1 tbsp freshly chopped parsley

NUTRITION INFORMATION: 750 kcal | 3130 kJ | 62 g protein | 43 g fat | 28 g carbohydrate

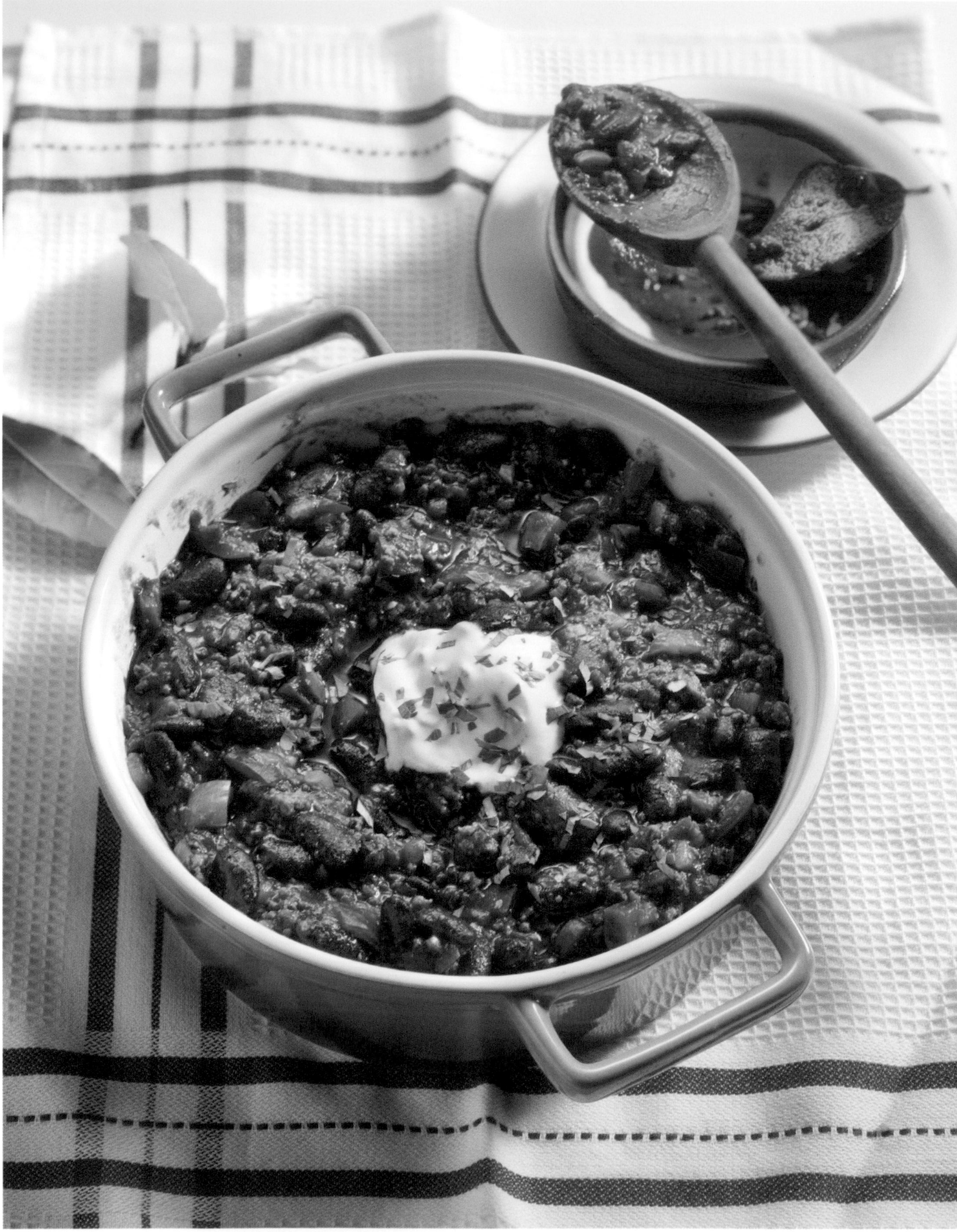

Chili con carne

Serves 4

PREPARATION TIME: approx. 40 minutes (plus cooking time)

Peel and finely chop the onions and garlic cloves. Halve and trim the peppers, then wash inside and out, pat dry, and dice finely. Cut the chilli in half lengthways and trim. Wash inside and out and chop finely. Rinse the beans in a sieve and leave to drain.

Heat the olive oil in a saucepan and brown the minced meat over a high heat. Break up with a wooden spoon until nice and crumbly. Add the onions, garlic, peppers and chilli. Sweat for a few moments. Stir in the tomato purée and cook for about 3 minutes. Pour over the beef stock. Add the peeled tomatoes and their juice. Stir in the bay leaf, sugar, paprika, cumin, oregano and a little salt and pepper. Bring to the boil, then reduce the heat and simmer gently for about 30 minutes.

Stir in the kidney beans, and simmer for about another hour. Check the seasoning, adding more salt, pepper and chilli if required. Spoon the chili con carne onto plates, and serve with a dollop of smooth soured cream and chopped coriander leaves if desired.

2 onions
2 garlic cloves
1 green pepper
1 red pepper
1 red chilli pepper
1 can of kidney beans (400 g)
4 tbsp olive oil
600 g minced beef
2 tbsp tomato purée
150 ml beef stock
1 can peeled tomatoes (400 g)
1 bay leaf
1 tsp brown sugar
2 tsp paprika powder
2 tsp cumin seeds
2 tsp dried oregano
salt
pepper
chilli powder

ADDITIONALLY
light soured cream and coriander leaves
if desired

NUTRITION INFORMATION: 620 kcal I 2590 kJ I 45 g protein I 35 g fat I 30 g carbohydrate

Fajitas

Serves 4

FOR THE MEAT AND THE MARINADE
600 g beef (flank)
1 papaya
1 small red onion
2 garlic cloves
1 green chilli pepper
2 tsp brown sugar
2 tbsp lemon juice
50 ml sherry
50 ml soy sauce

FOR THE GUACAMOLE
1 bunch coriander
1 red chilli pepper
2 garlic cloves
2 avocados
2 tbsp lime juice
salt
pepper

TO FINISH
1 red and 1 green pepper
1 red onion
½ bunch coriander
2 tbsp oil
salt
pepper
8 tortillas

PREPARATION TIME: approx. 50 minutes (plus marinating and baking time)

Rinse and pat dry the meat, and cut off any excess fat. Cut into bite-size, not-too-thin pieces. Wash, dry, peel and halve the papaya. Scoop out the seeds and roughly chop the flesh. Peel and roughly chop the onion and garlic cloves. Cut the chilli in half lengthways, then trim, wash and finely chop. Blend the papaya, onion, garlic, chilli, sugar, lemon juice, sherry and soy sauce in a blender. Combine with the meat and cover. Put in the refrigerator and marinate for at least 6 hours, and ideally overnight.

To make the guacamole, wash and shake dry the coriander, and finely chop the leaves. Halve the chilli pepper, then trim, wash and pat dry, and chop finely. Peel and crush the garlic. Peel the avocados. Remove the stones and mash the flesh in a bowl. Combine with the coriander, chilli, garlic and lime juice. Season well with salt and pepper.

To finish the fajitas, Pre-heat the oven to 180 °C (Gas Mark 4). Halve and trim the peppers, then wash and pat dry and cut into strips. Peel and thinly slice the red onion. Wash and shake dry the coriander and pluck off the leaves.

Remove the meat from the marinade, and use the back of a knife to scrape it off. Then heat the oil in a pan. Season the meat with salt and pepper, then brown all over in the hot oil. Remove, and sauté the pepper strips for a few moments. Combine in a bowl with the meat, onion rings and coriander.

Open out the tortillas and spread with half of the guacamole. Arrange the filling on top, then roll them up. Place on a parchment-lined baking sheet and bake for about 10 minutes. Remove from the oven, and serve with the remainder of the guacamole.

NUTRITION INFORMATION: 680 kcal | 2850 kJ | 43 g protein | 28 g fat | 60 g carbohydrate

BBQ chicken wings
with blue cheese dip

PREPARATION TIME: approx. 30 minutes (plus marinating and grilling time)

Halve the chicken wings at the joint. Wash, pat dry and place in a bowl. Peel and finely chop the garlic cloves. Combine with the ketchup, chilli sauce and honey. Pour over the chicken wings, making sure that they are completely covered in the marinade. Cover and leave in the refrigerator overnight, or for at least 6 hours.

Brush a grill rack with oil. Drain the chicken wings, then season with salt and pepper and grill until crisp.

To make the blue cheese dip, peel and finely chop the onion, and combine well with the cheese, mayonnaise, soured cream and lemon juice. Season well with salt and pepper, and serve on plates with the chicken wings and a few vegetable sticks. Goes well with crispy white bread or baked potatoes.

Alternatively, you can also bake the chicken wings in the oven. For that Pre-heat the oven to 180 °C (Gas Mark 4). Place the chicken wings on a parchment-lined baking sheet and bake in the oven for about 30 minutes. To finish, place under the grill for about 5 minutes until crisp.

Serves 4

20 chicken wings
3 garlic cloves
100 ml ketchup
100 ml sweet-and-sour chilli sauce
2 tbsp honey
salt
pepper

FOR THE DIP
1 onion
200 g blue cheese
250 g mayonnaise
250 g light soured cream
2 tbsp lemon juice
salt
pepper

ADDITIONALLY
mixed vegetable sticks for dipping
(e. g. carrots, celery and peppers)
oil for the rack

NUTRITION INFORMATION: 1000 kcal | 4190 kJ | 28 g protein | 90 g fat | 20 g carbohydrate

Baked lamb stew

Serves 4

2 onions
3 garlic cloves
2 carrots
125 g frozen peas
1 kg lamb (leg)
50 g streaky bacon
3 tbsp sunflower oil
salt
pepper
4 tbsp flour
150 ml dry white wine
200 ml lamb stock
1 can chopped tomatoes (400 g)
1 tbsp grated zest of 1 unwaxed orange
2 tbsp cognac
½ bunch flat-leafed parsley

PREPARATION TIME: approx. 45 minutes (plus cooking time)

Peel and finely chop the onions and garlic cloves. Wash, trim, peel and finely chop the carrots. Defrost the peas in a sieve. Trim the meat and cut into cubes of about 4 cm. Finely chop the bacon.

Pre-heat the oven to 180 °C (Gas Mark 4). Fry the bacon in a casserole until the fat runs and the bacon is crispy. Lift out and set aside. Pour the sunflower oil onto the bacon fat and heat. Season the diced lamb with salt and pepper, and dust with 2 tablespoons of flour. Fry on all sides in portions. Remove the meat, and dispose of all but about 2 tablespoons of the cooking liquid.

Lower the heat. Put the onions and carrots in the casserole. Fry for a few moments, then dust with the remainder of the flour. Pour over the white wine, then bring to the boil and deglaze. Stir in the garlic, lamb stock, tomatoes and orange zest. Add the meat, and bake, covered, in the middle of the oven for about 1 hour 20 minutes until done.

Remove the lid and stir in the cognac, and season well with salt and pepper. Stir in the peas and cook, uncovered, in the oven for a further 20 minutes. Wash and shake dry the parsley and chop the leaves.

Arrange the lamb stew on plates, sprinkle with the chopped parsley and serve with plain boiled potatoes.

NUTRITION INFORMATION: 620 kcal | 2590 kJ | 60 g protein | 20 g fat | 20 g carbohydrate

Roasted pork
with oranges

Serves 4

1 kg pork roast (leg, no crackling)
3 garlic cloves
2 sage stalks
½ bunch oregano
2 sprigs rosemary
2 tbsp sunflower oil
salt
pepper
300 ml freshly squeezed orange juice
125 g marmalade
4 tbsp hot mustard
2 tbsp brown sugar
6 tbsp orange liqueur
2 dashes Tabasco
50 g ice-cold butter

ADDITIONALLY
orange slices and fresh oregano to serve

PREPARATION TIME: approx. 40 minutes (plus cooking time)

Pre-heat the oven to 180 °C (Gas Mark 4). Wash and pat dry the roast, and cut off any excess fat. Peel the garlic cloves and cut into thin sticks.

Pierce the roast all over with a sharp knife, and spike with the garlic. Wash and shake dry the herbs, and finely chop the leaves and needles. Combine with the sunflower oil.

Season the meat with salt and pepper, and brush with the herb oil. Put on the drip pan and roast for about 1 hour. Baste frequently with a little orange juice.

Stir together the marmalade, mustard and sugar. Brush over the meat, and roast for a further 15 minutes. Remove from the oven and wrap in aluminium foil. Pour the cooking juices into a saucepan. Bring to the boil with the remainder of the orange juice, the orange liqueur and the Tabasco. Stir in flakes of the ice-cold butter to bind the sauce.

Thinly slice the roast, and serve garnished with a few fresh orange slices and oregano leaves. Croquettes are an excellent accompaniment.

NUTRITION INFORMATION: 640 kcal | 2685 kJ | 54 g protein | 30 g fat | 31 g carbohydrate

Dirty rice

Serves 4

250 g long-grain rice
650 ml chicken bouillon
2 onions
2 celery stalks
4 spring onions
1 green pepper
2 garlic cloves
100 g smoked bacon
250 g chicken livers
300 g pork fillet
2 tbsp olive oil
2 bay leaves
salt
pepper
½ tsp each of paprika powder and cumin seeds
dash of Tabasco
½ bunch flat-leafed parsley

ADDITIONALLY
lemon wedges to serve

PREPARATION TIME: approx. 40 minutes

Put the rice in a sieve. Rinse under running cold water and leave to drain. Put in a saucepan with the chicken bouillon. Bring to the boil and cook for about 15 minutes. Pour into a sieve and drain.

Peel and chop the onions. Wash, dry, trim and thinly dice the celery. Trim, wash and pat dry the spring onions, and thinly slice the white and light green parts. Halve the pepper and trim, then wash inside and out and chop finely. Peel and finely chop the garlic.

Chop the bacon into small cubes. Roughly chop the chicken livers. Wash and pat dry the pork fillet, and remove any remaining skin. Cut into small, bite-size strips.

Heat the bacon in a large pan until crisp. Add the liver and pork fillet and sauté. Add the oil and bay leaves. Now stir in the onions, celery, chopped pepper and garlic. Cook, stirring, for about 7 minutes. Season with salt, pepper, paprika and cumin, and finish with Tabasco.

Add the rice and combine well. Wash and shake dry the parsley and fold in with the spring onions. Arrange the rice on plates and serve with lemon wedges.

Spicy meat gumbo

Serves 4

4 chicken breasts
salt
pepper
400 g chorizo
4 slices of bacon
1 red onion
5 garlic cloves
1 green and 1 red pepper
4 celery stalks
4 spring onions
2 tbsp oil
4 tbsp flour
2 tsp dried thyme
3 bay leaves
400 ml chicken bouillon
1 can chopped tomatoes (400 g)
cayenne pepper

ADDITIONALLY
freshly cooked rice to serve

PREPARATION TIME: approx. 1 hour (plus cooking time)

Wash and pat dry the chicken breasts and cut into cubes. Season with salt and pepper. Slice the chorizo. Chop the bacon. Peel and chop the onion and garlic cloves. Halve and trim the peppers, then wash inside and out cut into small dice. Wash and dry the celery and spring onions, then trim and slice.

Heat the oil in a pan. Stir in the chicken, chorizo and bacon, and cook on all sides for about 10 minutes. Remove and set aside.

Add the onion, peppers and celery and cook, stirring, for about 4 minutes. Then dust with the flour. Cook, stirring, for about 15 minutes until golden. Now add the meat, garlic, thyme and bay leaves.

Pour over the chicken bouillon and tomatoes and bring to the boil, stirring continuously. Simmer gently over a low heat for about 40 minutes. Season well with salt, pepper and cayenne pepper. Arrange the gumbo on the rice and sprinkle with spring onions to serve.

NUTRITION INFORMATION: 710 kcal | 2950 kJ | 52 g protein | 47 g fat | 19 g carbohydrate

Chicken enchiladas

Serves 4

3 chicken breast fillets (approx. 600 g)
1 can kidney beans (400 g)
4 spring onions
1 green pepper
2 garlic cloves
2 tbsp sunflower oil
1 can chopped tomatoes (400 g)
100 ml chicken bouillon
2 dried chilli peppers
1 tbsp paprika powder
½ tsp dried oregano
1 tbsp ground cumin seeds
salt
pepper
pinch of sugar
250 g light soured cream
8 tortillas
200 g grated cheese

PREPARATION TIME: approx. 30 minutes (plus cooking and baking time)

Pre-heat the oven to 180 °C (Gas Mark 4). Wash and pat dry the chicken breasts and cut into small cubes 1.5 cm long. Rinse the beans in a sieve and drain. Wash, pat dry and trim the spring onions, then thinly slice the white and light green parts. Halve and trim the pepper, then wash inside and out, pat dry, and dice finely.

Heat half the oil in a saucepan and sauté the peeled garlic cloves over a medium heat for about 2 minutes. Pour in the chopped tomatoes and chicken bouillon, and stir. Crumble the dried chillies, and stir into the saucepan with the paprika powder, oregano and cumin seeds. Season with salt and pepper and stir in a little sugar. Bring to the boil and simmer, uncovered, for about 10 minutes. Remove from the hob.

Heat the remainder of the oil in a pan. Season the chicken with salt and pepper, and cook on all sides until light brown. Add the spring onions and pepper. Lower the heat slightly and simmer gently for a further 5 minutes. Stir in the beans, and season with salt and pepper. Remove from the hob.

Spread a little soured cream over the tortillas, and 2 tablespoons of tomato sauce over the cream. Arrange the filling on top, then sprinkle with a little cheese and roll the tortillas up. Place in an ovenproof dish. Stir the remainder of the soured cream into the tomato sauce and pour over the tortillas. Sprinkle over the remainder of the cheese, and bake in the middle of the oven for about 20 minutes. If any of the filling is left, warm it up again and serve it with the enchiladas.

NUTRITION INFORMATION: 1000 kcal I 4150 kJ I 64 g protein I 51 g fat I 67 g carbohydrate

Grilled club steak
with spicy potatoes and chimichurri

Serves 4

FOR THE CHIMICHURRI SAUCE

½ bunch flat-leafed parsley
1 bunch oregano
1 garlic clove
1 red chilli pepper
1 lime
75 ml olive oil
salt

FOR THE POTATOES

800 g waxy potatoes
5 sprigs rosemary
2 garlic cloves
approx. 1.5 l oil for deep-frying
1 tbsp paprika powder
1 tbsp curry powder
1 tsp salt
big pinch of sugar

FOR THE STEAKS

4 club steaks (off the bone approx.
250 g each, on the bone approx. 350 g)
salt
pepper
sunflower oil for the rack

PREPARATION TIME: approx. 40 minutes (plus time for deep-frying)

For the chimichurri, wash and shake dry the herbs and chop the leaves. Combine in a bowl. Peel the garlic and crush over the herbs. Halve the chilli, then trim, wash and chop finely. Squeeze the lime. Add both to the herbs with the olive oil and a little salt, and combine well.

Wash and peel the potatoes, and cut into not-too-thin sticks. Wash and pay dry the rosemary. Peel and quarter the garlic. Heat the rosemary and garlic in the deep-frying oil. When the oil reaches about 150 °C, scoop out the herbs with a slotted spoon as otherwise they will burn and turn bitter. Put the potatoes in the oil and deep-fry for about 15 minutes until golden. Lift out and drain. Then heat the oil to 180 °C.

Season the steaks with salt and pepper. Brush a grill rack with oil and grill the steaks over a high heat for about 3 minutes on each side. Turn only once so that a nice brown crust develops on the meat. Wrap the steaks in aluminium foil and leave to rest for about 5 minutes. During this time, put the potatoes back in the hot oil for about 4 minutes until they are golden and crisp. Lift out and drain, then combine in a bowl with the paprika and curry powder, salt and sugar. Unwrap the steaks, and serve with the potato chips and spicy sauce.

Variation: To prepare in the grill pan: Heat a little oil and fry the steaks over a high heat on both sides for about 3 minutes. Remove, and wrap in aluminium foil to rest for about 5 minutes. To cook the potatoes in the oven: Pre-heat it to 200 °C (Gas Mark 6). Combine the potatoes with 3 tablespoons of oil and 1 teaspoon of salt. Spread over a baking tray and bake in the oven for about 30 minutes. Sprinkle the garlic and rosemary over the top for the last 10 minutes. Remove the potatoes from the oven. Lift off the herbs, and dust the potatoes with curry and paprika powder, another pinch of salt and a pinch of sugar. This will stop them from becoming too crispy, but also makes them taste delicious.

NUTRITION INFORMATION: 960 kcal | 4020 kJ | 59 g protein | 65 g fat | 34 g carbohydrate

Midwestern meat loaf

Serves 4

1 stale bread roll
½ bunch flat-leafed parsley
3 basil stalks
3 spring onions
2 tbsp butter
600 g minced beef
100 g minced pork
100 g minced veal
1 tsp each of salt and pepper
1 egg
2 tbsp chilli sauce
2 tbsp ketchup
6 slices of bacon

ADDITIONALLY
olive oil for the dish

PREPARATION TIME: approx. 30 minutes (plus cooking time)

Pre-heat the oven to 200 °C (Gas Mark 6). Soften the roll in warm water. Wash and shake dry the herbs and chop the leaves. Wash, dry, trim and thinly slice the spring onions.

Heat the butter in a saucepan and sauté the spring onions over a low heat for about 5 minutes. Leave to cool.

Combine the meat in a bowl with the salt, pepper, egg, herbs, spring onions, chilli sauce and ketchup. Squeeze the roll out well, and shred into tiny pieces. Put in the bowl with the meat and other ingredients, and blend well.

Brush an ovenproof dish with oil. Shape the meat dough into a slightly elongated dumpling. Press 3 slices of the bacon onto the underside, and the other 3 on top. Put in the dish and bake for about 1 hour.

Cut the meat loaf into slices, and serve e. g. with mashed potatoes and green beans.

NUTRITION INFORMATION: 560 kcal | 2330 kJ | 45 g protein | 38 g fat | 10 g carbohydrate

Papaya chicken stew

Serves 4

PREPARATION TIME: approx. 30 minutes (plus cooking time)

Wash the lime in hot water, then dry. Thinly grate the zest and squeeze out the juice. Wash and shake dry the coriander and pluck off the leaves. Wash, dry, trim and thinly slice the spring onions. Peel and halve the papayas. Scoop out the seeds and dice the flesh. Peel and very finely chop the ginger and garlic cloves.

Wash and pat dry the chicken thighs and drumsticks. Sift the flour into a bowl, and combine with the spices and salt. Dust the chicken pieces with the seasoned flour.

Heat the sunflower and sesame oil in a casserole dish. Brown the chicken pieces all over in batches over a medium heat until they have acquired a pleasant colour. Remove the meat, and sauté the spring onions for about 3 minutes, stirring continuously. Add the garlic and ginger. Sauté for a few moments, then pour over the bouillon and deglaze the bottom of the dish. Stir in the sugar, lime juice and zest. Return the chicken pieces to the casserole dish. The chicken should just be covered by liquid, so add a little more if required.

Cover, and simmer gently over a low heat for about 30 minutes. Remove the lid and simmer for a further 15 minutes until the chicken is very tender. Finally, put the chopped papaya and the nuts in with the chicken and heat through. Season to taste with salt and pepper.

Arrange on plates with rice, and sprinkle with coriander to serve.

1 unwaxed lime
1 bunch coriander
6 spring onions
2 papayas
4 cm ginger
2 garlic cloves
4 chicken thighs
4 chicken drumsticks
75 g flour
1 tsp each of ground cumin, coriander, pepper, turmeric, cayenne pepper and salt
2 tbsp sunflower oil
1 tbsp sesame oil
approx. 1 l chicken bouillon
2 tbsp cane sugar
150 g macadamia nuts

ADDITIONALLY
rice to serve

NUTRITION INFORMATION: 780 kcal | 3260 kJ | 45 g protein | 53 g fat | 53 g carbohydrate

Veal parmigiana

Serves 4

1 bunch basil

1 onion

3 garlic cloves

3 anchovies

1 dried chilli pepper

5 tbsp olive oil

2 cans chopped tomatoes (400 g each)

salt

pepper

sugar

100 g Parmesan

175 g breadcrumbs

2 eggs

150 g flour

8 small thin veal escalopes
(approx. 100 g each)

2 mozzarella balls (125 g each)

ADDITIONALLY

olive oil for the dish

PREPARATION TIME: approx. 30 minutes (plus baking time)

Pre-heat the oven to 175 °C (Gas Mark 3.5). Wash and shake dry the basil and pluck off the leaves. Reserve a few to decorate, and roughly chop the rest. Peel and very finely chop the onion and garlic cloves. Rinse and chop the anchovies. Crumble the chilli.

Heat 1 tablespoon of olive oil in a saucepan and cook the onion for about 5 minutes, stirring continuously. Stir in the garlic and anchovies, and cook for a few moments. Then add the chopped tomatoes and crumbled chilli. Bring to the boil, then simmer for about 20 minutes. At the end, stir in the chopped basil, and season the sauce with salt, pepper and sugar.

Grate the Parmesan, and combine with the breadcrumbs in a deep plate. Whisk the eggs in a second deep plate. Sift the flour onto a third plate. Pat the escalopes dry, then season them with salt and pepper. Coat in the flour first, and tap off any excess. Then dip in the eggs, and after that in the breadcrumbs.

Heat the remainder of the oil in a pan, and fry the escalopes on both sides for about 3 minutes until golden. Remove, then place on paper towels to drain.

Brush a large ovenproof dish with olive oil. Pour in the tomato sauce, and arrange the escalopes on top. They need to go in beside each other, so use two gratin dishes if necessary. Chop the mozzarella and scatter over the escalopes. Bake in the oven for about 20 minutes until golden. Sprinkle with the basil to serve. Serve with crispy bread or spaghetti.

NUTRITION INFORMATION: 950 kcal | 3970 kJ | 76 g protein | 41 g fat | 67 g carbohydrate

Thanksgiving turkey

Serves 6-8

PREPARATION TIME: approx. 40 minutes (plus cooking time)

Pre-heat the oven to 180 °C (Gas Mark 4). Wash the turkey inside and out and pat dry. Season inside and out with salt and pepper. Chop the chorizo into cubes. Wash, dry and trim the celery and dice. Wash, pat dry and trim the spring onions, then thinly slice the white and light green parts. Chop the cornbread into small cubes.

Heat the olive oil in a pan and fry the chorizo until crisp. Add the celery and spring onions and cook for about 5 minutes. Put in a bowl. Roughly chop the walnuts and fry lightly in a pan without oil. Add to the bowl. Peel and quarter the apples, then cut out the cores and chop the flesh. Sprinkle with lemon juice. Add to the bread mixture with the cranberries. Combine all the ingredients and season with the thyme.

Fill the turkey with this stuffing. Secure the opening with wooden sticks, and tie together the wings and drumsticks with kitchen twine. Cover the breast and drumsticks with bacon. Put on the drip pan and roast in the middle of the oven for about 2 hours 30 minutes. Baste frequently with a little chicken bouillon.

Increase the temperature to 200 °C (Gas Mark 6). Remove the bacon. Cook the turkey for about another 30 minutes until crisp. Remove from the oven and strain the cooking juices into a saucepan. Keep the turkey warm in the switched-off oven. Bring the cooking juice to the boil and finish with the cream. Reduce slightly, and bind with a little gravy thickener if desired. Season with salt and pepper. Cut the turkey into portions, and arrange with the stuffing and a little of the gravy. Serve garnished with a sprig of fresh thyme.

1 small turkey (approx. 3.5 kg)
salt
pepper
100 g chorizo
3 celery stalks
2 spring onions
250 g cornbread
1 tbsp olive oil
75 g walnuts
4 apples
1 tbsp lemon juice
100 g dried cranberries
2 tsp freshly chopped thyme leaves
100 g bacon
500 ml chicken bouillon
200 ml cream
a little gravy thickener if desired

ADDITIONALLY
thyme sprigs to garnish

Fish and seafood

The coasts and rivers of the USA offer a tremendous variety of fish and seafood that are often transformed into fabulous dishes with fresh vegetables and fruit.

Jambalaya

Serves 4

400 g king prawns
400 g chicken breasts
200 g chorizo
100 g cooked ham
1 onion
2 garlic cloves
1 green pepper
1 red pepper
1 celery stalk
1 red chilli pepper
2 tbsp butter
400 g rice
1 can chopped tomatoes (400 g)
1 tsp dried thyme
1 bay leaf
1 l chicken bouillon
salt
pepper
cayenne pepper
sugar
2 tbsp freshly chopped parsley
4 lemon wedges

PREPARATION TIME: approx. 50 minutes (plus cooking time)

Devein the prawns and rinse under running cold water. Pat dry, then cover and chill until required. Rinse and pat dry the chicken breasts and cut into cubes. Cut the chorizo into not-too-thin slices. Chop the ham.

Peel and chop the onion and garlic cloves. Halve and trim the peppers, then wash inside and out, pat dry, and chop into cubes. Wash and trim the celery, and cut into thin slices. Halve the chilli pepper, then trim, wash and chop.

Fry the chorizo in a pan over a medium heat for about 10 minutes until the fat starts to run and the sausage turns brown. Lift out and set aside. Cook the chicken in the juices over a high heat for about 5 minutes. Lift out. Add the chopped ham and cook for about 3 minutes, stirring continuously. Lift out.

Melt the butter in a saucepan and sauté the onion for about 5 minutes, stirring continuously. Then stir in the chopped pepper, celery, chilli and garlic. Sauté for a further 3 minutes. Stir in the chicken, chorizo, ham and rice. Add the chopped tomatoes and herbs, then pour in the chicken bouillon and bring to the boil.

Lower the heat and simmer the mixture gently for about 30 minutes until the rice is cooked. Then fold in the prawns, and cook until they turn pink.

Season well with salt, pepper, cayenne pepper and sugar. Arrange on plates and sprinkle with parsley. Serve with a lemon wedge on each portion.

NUTRITION INFORMATION: 860 kcal | 3600 kJ | 63 g protein | 28 g fat | 87 g carbohydrate

Poached salmon
with dill sauce

Serves 4

PREPARATION TIME: approx. 25 minutes

Wash and pat dry the salmon fillets. Wash, pat dry and finely chop the dill.

Bring the fish stock to the boil with the white wine and lemon slices in a saucepan that is big enough to hold the salmon as well. Season the liquid with salt and pepper and lower the heat.

Carefully put the salmon fillets in the liquid. The fillets should be completely submerged in the liquid. Add a little more liquid if required. Poach the salmon in the liquid, which should be very hot but not boiling, for about 10 minutes.

Melt the butter in a saucepan and stir in the cornflour. Sauté, stirring, for about 5 minutes, then measure out 250 ml of the fish liquid. Pour into the butter and cornflour mixture and whisk to prevent any lumps from forming. Add the cream and bring to the boil. Season with salt and pepper and stir in the dill.

Serve the salmon with the sauce, a little fresh dill and 1 lemon wedge. Goes well with plain boiled potatoes and steamed vegetables, such as broccoli.

4 salmon fillets (approx. 250 g each)
1 bunch dill
500 ml fish stock (jar)
400 ml dry white wine
2 slices of 1 unwaxed lemon
salt
pepper
2 tbsp butter
2 tbsp cornflour
75 ml cream

ADDITIONALLY
lemon wedges and fresh dill to garnish
boiled potatoes and steamed broccoli to serve

NUTRITION INFORMATION: 690 kcal ‖ 2870 kJ ‖ 46 g protein ‖ 45 g fat ‖ 7 g carbohydrate

Shrimp Creole

Serves 4

FOR THE PRAWNS

1 kg king prawns (ready-to-use)
2 garlic cloves
2 cm ginger
2 limes
1 tsp ground cayenne pepper
12 tbsp olive oil
2 green peppers
2 spring onions
salt
pepper

FOR THE RELISH

1 bunch coriander
1 papaya
1 mango
1 red chilli pepper
1 lime
1 tbsp olive oil
1 tsp paprika powder
salt
pepper
sugar

ADDITIONALLY

rice to serve

PREPARATION TIME: approx. 40 minutes (plus marinating time)

Devein the prawns. Rinse them under cold water, then pat them dry. Peel and very finely chop the garlic cloves and ginger. Squeeze the limes. Combine with the prawns, ginger, garlic, cayenne pepper and 10 tablespoons of olive oil. Cover and marinate in the refrigerator for about 1 hour.

Now make the relish. Wash and shake dry the coriander and chop the leaves. Wash and peel the papaya and mango. Halve the papaya and scoop out the seeds. Chop the flesh into small cubes. Cut the mango flesh off the stone and cube. Cut the chilli in half and trim. Wash inside and out and chop finely. Squeeze the lime. Combine with the olive oil, paprika powder, a little salt and pepper and a pinch of sugar. Leave to stand at room temperature until ready to serve.

Halve the green peppers and trim, then wash inside and out and chop finely. Trim, wash and dry the spring onions, then slice into rings.

Heat the remainder of the oil in a pan. Remove the prawns from the marinade and pat dry. Fry with the peppers and spring onions. Pour over a little of the marinade and simmer for about 5 minutes. Season to taste with salt and pepper. Arrange on rice and serve with the relish.

NUTRITION INFORMATION: 490 kcal | 2050 kJ | 48 g protein | 22 g fat | 23 g carbohydrate

Omelette Gordon Bennett

Serves 4

8 spring onions
400 g smoked haddock (alternatively smoked trout)
1 unwaxed lemon
8 eggs
100 ml milk
½ tsp salt
pepper
80 g Parmesan
4 tbsp butter
1 bunch chives

ADDITIONALLY
Parmesan to sprinkle

PREPARATION TIME: approx. 25 minutes

Trim, wash and pat dry the spring onions. Cut the white and light green sections into thin rings. Remove any remaining bones from the fish. Break the fish into bite-size pieces. Wash the lemon in hot water, then dry and grate the zest.

Put the eggs and milk in a bowl. Add the salt and a little pepper. Finely grate the Parmesan and add to the eggs. Whisk lightly with a fork.

Melt the butter in two pans over a medium heat. Divide the spring onions and fish between the two pans. Simmer gently for about 5 minutes, stirring well, until coated all round with the butter. Pour half of the egg mixture in each pan. Cook over a medium heat for 7 minutes until set on the top. Meanwhile, wash, pat dry and chop the chives.

Cut the omelettes in half straight away and arrange on plates. Grate over the Parmesan and sprinkle with the chives. Serve with a fresh salad and crispy white bread.

NUTRITION INFORMATION: 450 kcal | 1860 kJ | 44 g protein | 27 g fat | 7 g carbohydrate

Surf ´n´ turf gumbo

Serves 4

PREPARATION TIME: approx. 1 hour (plus cooking time)

Devein the prawns, then rinse under running cold water and pat dry. Rinse and pat dry the monkfish, then cut into bite-size pieces. Squeeze the lime. Combine the lime juice, prawns and monkfish in a bowl.

Wash and pat dry the lamb and cut into bite-size chunks. Cut the chorizo into slices. Wash, pat dry and dice the celery. Halve and trim the peppers, then wash inside and out and pat dry. Then cut into bite-size pieces. Peel and chop the onions and garlic cloves.

Season the lamb with salt, pepper and cayenne pepper and dust with 2 tablespoons of flour. Heat the oil in a pan and fry all round until golden, then remove from the pan.

Heat the dripping. Gradually add the remainder of the flour, stirring continuously. Fry slowly in the fat for about 20 minutes until it turns a rich brown. (This mixture is called a roux, and is used a great deal in the Southern States.) Remove the saucepan from the hob and stir in the onions, peppers and celery. Put back on the heat and continue cooking for about 3 minutes, stirring continuously. Pour in the chicken bouillon. Bring to the boil, stirring continuously.

Stir in the lamb and chorizo. Reduce the heat, and cook gently for about 2 hours. Keep scooping off any oil that floats on the surface – it is important that you do this, as otherwise the dish will be too oily. Stir in the garlic and thyme about 30 minutes before the end of the cooking time.

Put the prawns and monkfish in the saucepan, and cook for about 10 minutes. Then season well with salt, pepper, cayenne pepper and Tabasco. Arrange on plates with rice, and serve.

16 king prawns
200 g monkfish
1 lime
400 g lamb fillet
200 g chorizo
2 celery stalks
2 green peppers
4 onions
3 garlic cloves
salt
pepper
cayenne pepper
100 g flour
2 tbsp vegetable oil
200 g pork dripping
1.5 l chicken bouillon
1 tbsp freshly chopped thyme
Tabasco

ADDITIONALLY
rice to serve

NUTRITION INFORMATION: 580 kcal | 2430 kJ | 60 g protein | 27 g fat | 35 g carbohydrate

Maryland crab cakes
with tartar sauce

Serves 4

FOR THE CRAB CAKES

2 shallots
½ bunch flat-leafed parsley
75 g white bread
75 ml milk
500 g crab flesh
1 egg
3 tbsp mayonnaise
1 tsp mustard
½ tsp cream of tartar
salt
pepper
2 tbsp flour
2 tbsp butter
2 tbsp oil

FOR THE TARTAR SAUCE

1 pickled gherkin
1 tbsp capers
2 shallots
1 bunch chives
150 ml mayonnaise
200 g light soured cream
½ tsp mustard
salt
pepper
Tabasco
dash of lemon juice

PREPARATION TIME: approx. 30 minutes (plus time to chill and cook)

Peel and finely chop the shallots. Wash and spin dry the parsley and finely chop the leaves. Tear the white bread into pieces and soak in the milk. Finely chop the crab flesh.

Stir together the egg, mayonnaise and mustard. Add the white bread with the milk, shallots and parsley. Stir in the crab flesh and cream of tartar. Then season with salt and pepper.

Shape this mixture into 8 small patties. Put on a plate, cover with clingfilm and chill in the refrigerator for about 1 hour. Meanwhile, prepare the tartar sauce.

Finely chop the gherkin. Chop the capers. Peel and very finely chop the shallots. Wash and pat dry the chives and cut into little rolls. Stir together with the mayonnaise, soured cream and mustard. Season with salt, pepper, Tabasco and lemon juice.

Dust the crab cakes with flour. Heat the butter and oil in a pan. Fry the crab cakes over a medium heat for about 6 minutes on each side. Remove from the pan and drain on kitchen paper. Serve with the tartar sauce.

NUTRITION INFORMATION: 710 kcal | 3950 kJ | 26 g protein | 59 g fat | 19 g carbohydrate

Tuna noodle casserole

Serves 4

PREPARATION TIME: approx. 30 minutes (plus baking time)

Cook the ribbon noodles in plenty of boiling salter water. Pour off the water, rinse under running cold water, and leave in a colander to drain. Then pre-heat the oven to 200 °C (Gas Mark 6). Grease a gratin dish with butter. Peel and finely chop the onion and garlic. Wipe the mushrooms with damp kitchen paper, then trim and cut into slices. Defrost the peas.

Melt the butter in a saucepan. Sauté the onion in it for about 5 minutes. Add the garlic, and cook for about 2 minutes. Dust with the flour and fry for about 3 minutes. Pour over the milk and chicken stock and stir well to prevent any lumps from forming. Bring to the boil, stirring continuously.

Add the mushrooms and peas, and simmer for about 5 minutes. Remove from the hob and stir in the noodles and soured cream. Grate and combine the two cheeses. Stir in half the cheese. Drain the tuna in a sieve. Break up with a fork and fold into the noodles. Season to taste with salt and pepper. Put in the gratin dish.

Combine the remainder of the cheese with the breadcrumbs and sprinkle over the top. Top with flakes of butter. Bake in the middle of the oven for about 35 minutes until golden. Serve with a fresh green salad.

300 g thick (ribbon) noodles with egg
salt
1 onion
1 garlic clove
200 g button mushrooms
125 g frozen peas
20 g butter
20 g flour
125 ml milk
150 ml chicken stock
1 pot light soured cream (200 g)
200 g cheddar
75 g Parmesan
2 cans tuna fish (in its own juice)
pepper
2 tbsp breadcrumbs
2 tbsp flaked butter

ADDITIONALLY
butter for the dish

NUTRITION INFORMATION: 910 kcal ‖ 3830 kJ ‖ 60 g protein ‖ 44 g fat ‖ 69 g carbohydrate

Salmon with pumpkin crust

Serves 4

1 small Hokkaido pumpkin (approx. 800 g)
100 g pumpkin seeds
4 shallots
1 leek
2 tbsp oil
salt
pepper
1 pot light soured cream (200 g)
½ dried chilli pepper
4 salmon fillets (approx. 200 g each)
1 lemon
100 g cheddar

ADDITIONALLY
butter for the dish

PREPARATION TIME: approx. 30 minutes (plus baking time)

Pre-heat the oven to 180 °C (Gas Mark 4) and butter the inside of a gratin dish. Wash the pumpkin and cut in half. Scoop out the seeds and fibres. Cut the pumpkin into wedges and peel. (Although you can eat the skin of a hokkaido pumpkin, it tastes a little floury.)

Weight out 500 g of the flesh and grate it on a food grater. Chop the pumpkin seeds to about medium fine. Peel and finely chop the shallots. Wash, dry and trim the leek, and chop the white and pale green section.

Fry the pumpkin seeds in a pan without oil until the aroma just starts to fill the air. Then put in a bowl. Pour the oil into the pan and sauté the shallots and leek for about 6 minutes, stirring continuously. Add the pumpkin flesh and cook for a further 5 minutes. Season with salt and pepper. Stir in the soured cream and crumble over the dried chilli. Stir in the pumpkin seeds.

Wash and pat dry the salmon fillets, and remove any remaining bones. Wash and pat dry the lemon. Cut in half lengthways. Cut one half into 4 wedges. Squeeze the other half over the fish.

Sprinkle a little salt and pepper over the fish. Place skin side down in the gratin dish. Spread with the pumpkin mixture. Grate the cheddar and arrange over the fish.

Bake in the middle of the oven for about 25 minutes. Serve with little rösti or plain boiled potatoes.

NUTRITION INFORMATION: 800 kcal ‖ 3360 kJ ‖ 60 g protein ‖ 57 g fat ‖ 14 g carbohydrate

Coconut seafood burger

Serves 4

2 cm ginger
2 garlic cloves
1 green chilli pepper
1 unwaxed lime
250 g shrimps (ready-to-use)
250 g redfish fillet
250 g salmon fillet without the skin
1–2 tbsp grated coconut
2 tbsp curry powder
1 tbsp soy sauce
salt
pepper
1 egg
1–2 tbsp breadcrumbs
4 lettuce leaves
1 bunch chives
1 red onion
4 tbsp mayonnaise
4 tbsp light soured cream
2 tbsp sunflower oil
4 hamburger buns

PREPARATION TIME: approx. 40 minutes

Pre-heat the oven to 180 °C (Gas Mark 4). Peel and very finely grate the ginger and garlic cloves. Halve the chilli, then trim, wash and chop very finely. Wash the lime in hot water, then dry and grate the zest. Squeeze out the juice. Devein the shrimps. Rinse under cold water and pat dry. Wash and pat dry the fish, and carefully remove any remaining bones.

Chop the fish and shrimps very small. Put half in the container of a blender. Add 1 tablespoon of lime juice, and blend for just a few moments until still quite "chunky". Put in with the finely chopped fish. Add the ginger, garlic, chilli and grated coconut. Season with 1 tablespoon of curry powder, the soy sauce, salt and pepper. Add the egg and 1–2 tablespoons of breadcrumbs, and knead until smooth. Chill until ready to use.

Wash, trim and spin dry the lettuce leaves. Wash and pat dry the chives, then slice into little rolls. Peel the red onion and cut into very thin rings.

Stir together the mayonnaise, soured cream, 1 tablespoon of curry powder, the lime zest and the remainder of the lime juice. Season with salt and pepper and fold in the chopped chives.

Heat the oil in a pan. Shape the fish mixture into 4 patties, and fry each one for about 7 minutes on both sides until golden. Meanwhile, halve the buns and toast them in the oven for about 5 minutes with the cut sides up.

Spread 1 tablespoon of sauce over each of the bottom halves. Place 1 salad leaf on each. Put a seafood burger on each salad leaf. Arrange the red onion rings on top, and then spread with the remainder of the sauce. Place the top half of the buns on top, and serve immediately. Goes well with fries.

NUTRITION INFORMATION: 550 kcal | 2300 kJ | 43 g protein | 29 g fat | 29 g carbohydrate

Vegetarian dishes

American cooking also has plenty to keep vegetarians happy. The classics macaroni and cheese, burritos and tacos with brightly coloured vegetable fillings or a juicy four cheese pizza leave nothing to be desired.

Macaroni and cheese

Serves 4

PREPARATION TIME: approx. 25 minutes (plus baking time)

Pre-heat the oven to 200 °C (Gas Mark 6). Grease a gratin dish with butter. Cook the macaroni in accordance with the manufacturer's instructions in plenty of boiling salted water until al dente. Drain. Grate the two cheeses.

Melt the butter in a pan. Sprinkle over the flour and cook for about 2 minutes. Gradually add the milk, stirring continuously to prevent any lumps from forming. Bring to the boil, still stirring, then simmer for about 4 minutes. Remove from the hob. Season with salt, white pepper and grated nutmeg. Stir in the mustard, mascarpone and grated cheese.

Combine the pasta in a bowl with the cheese. Pour into the gratin dish. Grate the Parmesan. Combine with the breadcrumbs and sprinkle over the pasta. Bake in the middle of the oven for about 20 minutes until golden. Serve with a fresh green salad.

400 g macaroni
salt
200 g cheddar
200 g Gouda
3 tbsp butter
2 tbsp flour
400 ml milk
white pepper
grated nutmeg
2 tsp mustard
50 g mascarpone
50 g Parmesan
3 tbsp breadcrumbs

ADDITIONALLY
butter for the dish

Tacos with beans

Serves 4

1 can kidney beans (500 g)
1 green pepper
1 red pepper
4 spring onions
2 garlic cloves
1 red chilli pepper
4 tomatoes
100 g black olives
½ bunch flat-leafed parsley
3 tbsp olive oil
salt
pepper
2 tbsp ketchup
3 tbsp chilli sauce
1 tsp ground cumin seed
6 iceberg lettuce leaves
150 g cheddar
125 g crème fraîche
8 taco shells

PREPARATION TIME: approx. 40 minutes (plus cooling time)

Pre-heat the oven to 180 °C (Gas Mark 4). Rinse the beans in a sieve and leave to drain. Halve and trim the peppers, then wash inside and out and cut into thin strips. Wash, dry and trim the spring onions. Cut the white and light green sections into thin rings. Peel and finely chop the garlic cloves. Halve the chilli pepper, then trim, wash and chop small. Wash and dry the tomatoes. Cut out the stalks and cut the tomatoes in half. Scoop out the seeds with a spoon and dice the flesh. Chop the olives. Wash and shake dry the parsley and chop the leaves.

Heat the olive oil in a pan. Sauté half the spring onions and the garlic over a low heat for about 3 minutes, stirring continuously. Add the peppers, chilli and tomatoes. Simmer for a further 8 minutes. Stir in the parsley, beans and olives. Season with salt and pepper and stir in the ketchup, chilli sauce and cumin. Bring to the boil, then remove from the heat and leave to cool.

Wash and spin dry the iceberg lettuce, then trim it and cut the leaves into strips. Grate the cheese. Stir a little salt into the crème fraîche.

Heat the taco shells in the oven for about 3 minutes. Spoon the bean mixture into the shells. Top with the crème fraîche, the grated cheese and the remainder of the spring onions, and serve immediately.

NUTRITION INFORMATION: 610 kcal | 2540 kJ | 16 g protein | 42 g fat | 42 g carbohydrate

Vegetable jambalaya

Serves 4

PREPARATION TIME: approx. 30 minutes (plus cooking time)

Put the rice in a sieve and rinse, then leave to drain. Peel and finely chop the onion and garlic cloves. Halve the chillies, then trim, wash and chop finely. Wash, dry and trim the celery and cut into slices. Halve and trim the peppers, then wash inside and out, pat dry, and cut into bite-size pieces. Wash, trim and slice the courgettes.

Heat the olive oil in a large saucepan. Sauté the onion over a medium heat for about 5 minutes, stirring continuously. Then add the garlic, peppers, chilli pepper, celery and courgettes, and simmer for about 3 minutes. Season with salt and pepper. Add the bay leaves, oregano and thyme, paprika powder and tomato purée, and stir in.

Wash, dry, trim and dice the aubergine. Put in the saucepan with the tomatoes, vegetable bouillon and rice. Stir well, and simmer gently over a low heat for about 25 minutes. Season with salt, pepper, brown sugar and a little Tabasco, and sprinkle with chopped parsley to serve.

220 g long-grain rice
1 onion
2 garlic cloves
1 red chilli pepper
2 celery stalks
1 red and 1 green pepper
2 small courgettes
3 tbsp olive oil
salt
pepper
2 bay leaves
½ tsp dried oregano
½ tsp dried thyme
2 tsp sweet paprika powder
1 tbsp tomato purée
1 aubergine
1 can chopped tomatoes (400 g)
500 ml vegetable bouillon
brown sugar
Tabasco

ADDITIONALLY
chopped parsley to garnish

NUTRITION INFORMATION: 350 kcal | 1450 kJ | 9 g protein | 9 g fat | 56 g carbohydrate

Burritos mexicana
with salsa

Serves 4

FOR THE BURRITOS
400 g firm tofu
2 garlic cloves
1 tbsp paprika powder
cayenne pepper
ground cumin seed
4 tbsp olive oil
1 onion
1 can kidney beans (500 g)
1 can sweetcorn (500 g)
1 large green pepper
8 iceberg lettuce leaves
75 ml vegetable bouillon
8 tortillas

FOR THE SALSA
1 bunch coriander
1 unwaxed lime
4 spring onions
500 g tomatoes
1 red chilli pepper
salt
pepper

ADDITIONALLY
guacamole (recipe on page 44)

PREPARATION TIME: approx. 1 hour

Cut the tofu into small cubes. Peel and finely chop the garlic cloves. Mix the tofu in a bowl with half the garlic, the paprika powder, 1 teaspoon each of cayenne pepper and ground cumin and 2 tablespoons of olive oil. Cover and place in the refrigerator to marinate for at least 1 hour.

Meanwhile, prepare the salsa. Wash and shake dry the coriander and chop the leaves. Squeeze the lime. Wash, dry and trim the spring onions, then slice the white and light green parts. Wash the tomatoes. Cut out the stalks and remove the seeds. Chop the flesh. Halve the chilli pepper, then trim, wash and chop. Combine everything in a bowl and season with salt and pepper. Prepare the guacamole as explained in the recipe on page 44.

Pre-heat the oven to 180 °C (Gas Mark 4). Peel and chop the onion. Rinse the beans in a sieve and drain. Put the sweetcorn in a second sieve. Again, rinse and drain. Halve and trim the pepper, then wash inside and out and cut into strips. Wash, trim and spin dry the lettuce, and cut into strips.

Heat 1 tablespoon of oil in a pan and sauté the onion for 5 minutes. Add the garlic and stir in quickly. Put in a blender container with the red beans and vegetable bouillon, and blend briefly; it should still be quite chunky. Season with salt, pepper, cayenne pepper and cumin seeds.

Heat the remainder of the oil in a pan. Remove the tofu cubes from the marinade. Season with salt, and fry on all sides in the hot oil over a medium heat until golden. Heat the tortillas in the oven for about 3 minutes.

Open the tortillas. Spread the guacamole on one side and the kidney bean purée on the other. Arrange the sweetcorn, sliced peppers, tofu and lettuce on top. Roll up and serve with the tomato salsa.

NUTRITION INFORMATION: 580 kcal | 2420 kJ | 33 g protein | 21 g fat | 62 g carbohydrate

Four cheese pizza

Serves 4

FOR THE PASTRY
400 g flour
10 g fresh yeast
salt
4 tbsp olive oil

FOR THE TOPPING
1 bunch basil
2 garlic cloves
150 ml puréed tomatoes
salt
pepper
pinch of sugar
250 g mozzarella
80 g Gorgonzola
50 g Parmesan
50 g pecorino

ADDITIONALLY
flour for the work surface and to dust
olive oil for drizzling
dried oregano for sprinkling

PREPARATION TIME: approx. 30 minutes (plus standing and baking time)

Stir together 250 g flour and 260 ml cold water. Then crumble over the yeast and add 1 tablespoon of salt. Stir until you have a smooth dough that is starting to bubble. Cover and leave to rest for about 30 minutes. Now slowly – it should take about 5 minutes – stir in the remainder of the flour and the olive oil. Stir again. Cover the bowl and leave to rest for a further 20 minutes. Then place in the refrigerator for at least 4 hours, and ideally overnight.

Pre-heat the oven to 220 °C (Gas Mark 7). Line two baking trays with baking parchment. Wash and shake dry the basil. Pluck off the leaves and chop. Peel the garlic cloves and crush into the tomatoes. Stir in the chopped basil. Season with salt, pepper and sugar.

Chop the mozzarella and Gorgonzola separately, and grate the Parmesan and pecorino separately. Take the dough out of the refrigerator and knead thoroughly on a floured worktop. Divide into 4 equally-sized pieces. Roll each piece out into a circle about half the size of the baking tray so you can put 2 pizzas together on each tray.

Arrange the dough circles on the trays and spread with the tomato sauce. Then sprinkle first with the pecorino and Parmesan, then the Gorgonzola and mozzarella. Drizzle with olive oil and dust with a little pepper.

Bake each tray on the bottom runner of the oven for about 20 minutes. Remove from the oven, and sprinkle with a little dried oregano to serve.

NUTRITION INFORMATION: 770 kcal | 3230 kJ | 33 g protein | 38 g fat | 75 g carbohydrate

Desserts

The Americans are undeniably sweet-toothed, and the desserts are substantial and delicious to prove this — Maple flan, NY cheesecake, Pumpkin pie and doughnuts are the favourites.

Maple flan

Serves 4

175 ml maple syrup
3 eggs
1 egg yolks
150 ml milk
150 ml cream
1 sachet vanilla sugar
pinch of salt

ADDITIONALLY
butter for the tins
fresh berries and croquant to serve

PREPARATION TIME: approx. 20 minutes (plus cooking, cooling and chilling time)

Pre-heat the oven to 150 °C (Gas Mark 2). Lightly butter 4 small ovenproof dishes (approx. 8 cm diameter).

Measure out 100 ml of the maple syrup. Put in a saucepan and reduce to 70 ml, stirring continuously. Remove from the heat and leave until lukewarm.

Whisk the eggs, egg yolk and the remainder of the maple syrup until thick and fluffy. Heat the milk, cream, vanilla sugar and salt in a saucepan. Gradually whisk in to the egg and maple syrup mixture.

Spoon the reduced maple syrup into the tins. Carefully pour over the custard mixture without disturbing the maple syrup on the bases.

Put the tins in the oven drip pan and pour in hot water to halfway up the moulds. Bake in the middle of the oven for about 40 minutes. Leave to cool, then cover and refrigerate for at least 3 hours.

Finally, tip the flans out onto dessert plates and garnish with fresh berries and croquant to serve.

NUTRITION INFORMATION: 360 kcal I 1490 kJ I 8 g protein I 19 g fat I 38 g carbohydrate

Serves 4

4 small ripe bananas
4 tbsp butter
100 g brown sugar
3 tbsp banana liqueur
dash of lemon juice
60 ml Jamaica rum
pig pinch of cinnamon

ADDITIONALLY

vanilla ice cream and whipped cream
to serve

Bananas Foster

PREPARATION TIME: approx. 15 minutes

Peel the bananas and cut in half lengthways. Melt the butter in a large pan. Pour in the brown sugar and stir well. Allow to caramelise lightly, then stir in the liqueur and a little lemon juice.

Heat the rum in a second saucepan. Put the bananas in the pan. Carefully fry all over for about 2 minutes, then glaze with the caramel. Pour over the hot rum. Set alight and flambé.

Sprinkle over the cinnamon while the flame is still burning. Wait until the flames have gone out, then arrange the bananas on plates. The bananas are delicious with 1 ball of vanilla ice cream and a little whipped cream.

NUTRITION INFORMATION: 350 kcal | 1450 kJ | 2 g protein | 8 g fat |
52 g carbohydrate

NY cheesecake

Makes 14 slices
(1 springform tin, 24 cm diameter)

200 g digestive biscuits
80 g butter
1 tbsp icing sugar
1 unwaxed lemon
1 kg cream cheese
300 g sugar
350 g traditional soured cream
1 tsp vanilla extract
6 eggs
3 tbsp cornflour

ADDITIONALLY
butter for the springform tin
fresh forest berries to serve

PREPARATION TIME: approx. 30 minutes (plus cooling, chilling and baking time)

Butter the base and sides of the springform tin. Crumble the digestive biscuits. The best way to do this is to put the biscuits in a freezer bag and roll over them with a rolling pin until you are left with fine crumbs. Put the crumbs in a bowl. Melt the butter and pour over the crumbs with the icing sugar. Combine well, then spread over the base of the springform tin and press down well. Cover and chill for about 30 minutes.

Pre-heat the oven to 140 °C (Gas Mark 1). Wash the lemon in hot water and dry. Finely grate the zest and squeeze out the juice. Stir both together in a bowl with the cream cheese and soured cream until smooth. Stir in the vanilla extract, then add the eggs individually. Make sure that the mixture does not get foamy. The cake should be creamy and dense when done. Set the hand mixer at the lowest setting, and combine everything slowly and carefully. Sift over the cornflour and combine well.

Pour the cream cheese mixture over the biscuit base. Smooth the surface, and bake in the middle of the oven for about 1 hour 10 minutes. The cake is done when the surface is a soft brown, and the cream filling only moves very slightly when gently shaken, rather than forming waves. It will become firmer as it cools. Leave the cake in the oven with the door slightly open for about 2 hours. Then cover and place in the refrigerator for at least 4 hours, and ideally overnight. Serve with fresh forest berries and dusted with icing sugar.

NUTRITION INFORMATION: 560 kcal | 2340 kJ | 12 g protein | 42 g fat | 34 g carbohydrate

Key lime pie

Makes 14 slices
(1 springform tin, 24 cm diameter)

225 g digestive biscuits
125 g butter
6 unwaxed limes
6 eggs
400 ml sweetened condensed milk
2 tbsp cornflour
salt
180 g sugar
pig pinch of cream of tartar

ADDITIONALLY
butter for the springform tin

PREPARATION TIME: approx. 35 minutes (plus chilling, baking and cooling time)

Finely crush the digestive biscuits. The best way to do this is to put the biscuits in a freezer bag and roll over them with a rolling pin until you are left with fine crumbs. Then put in a bowl. Melt the butter in a saucepan and pour over the biscuit crumbs. Combine well. Butter the base and sides of the springform tin. Cover the base of the springform tin with the crumb mixture and press down well. Make a little rim around the sides. Cover and chill for about 30 minutes.

Pre-heat the oven to 180 °C (Gas Mark 4). Wash the limes in hot water and dry, then thinly grate the zest of 3 of them. Squeeze the limes and measure out 125 ml juice.

Separate the eggs. Put the egg whites in the refrigerator. Whisk the egg yolks with the condensed milk for at least 5 minutes until thick and creamy. Then stir in the lime zest and juice. Sift over the cornflour and whisk until smooth. Pour the cream over the crumb base, and bake in the middle of the oven for about 30 minutes.

Just before the end of the baking time, whisk the egg whites with a little salt until they are just foamy. Slowly whisk in the sugar. Continue whisking until the sugar crystals have dissolved completely and the mixture is quite stiff. Then stir in the cream of tartar. Increase the temperature of the oven to 250 °C (Gas Mark 9).

Fetch the pie out of the oven and spoon the meringue mixture over it in clouds. Finish baking on the bottom runner for about 4 minutes, until the peaks of the meringue are nice and brown but not burnt. Leave the pie to cool. Do not refrigerate, and serve on the same day.

NUTRITION INFORMATION: 350 kcal | 1450 kJ | 7 g protein | 16 g fat | 42 g carbohydrate

Blueberry pancakes

Serves 4

250 g flour
1 tbsp sugar
pinch of salt
4 eggs
100 ml milk
250 ml buttermilk
300 g fresh blueberries
2 tsp baking soda
2 tsp baking powder

ADDITIONALLY
butter for baking
maple syrup for drizzling

PREPARATION TIME: approx. 20 minutes (plus standing and baking time)

Pre-heat the oven to 100 °C (Gas Mark 0.5 at most). Line a baking tray with baking parchment. Put the flour in a bowl. Add the sugar, salt, eggs, milk and buttermilk. Whisk until smooth, then cover and leave to stand for at least 30 minutes.

Wash and carefully pat dry the blueberries. Then sift the baking soda and baking powder over the batter and whisk until smooth. Carefully fold in the blueberries.

Melt a little butter in a pan, and ladle portions of the batter into the pan. Smooth the surface, and cook little pancakes over a medium heat. When the underside is golden (after about 6 minutes), turn and repeat on the other side. Then place on the baking tray and keep warm. Repeat until all the batter has been used.

Arrange the pancakes on plates and drizzle with maple syrup to serve.

NUTRITION INFORMATION: 370 kcal ‖ 1560 kJ ‖ 17 g protein ‖ 8 g fat ‖ 57 g carbohydrate

Apple Brown Betty

Serves 4

4 stale bread rolls
100 g butter
75 g brown sugar
big pinch of cinnamon
1 tsp grated zest of 1 unwaxed lemon
750 g tart apples
1 tbsp lemon juice
50 ml apple juice

ADDITIONALLY
butter for the dish
whipped cream and vanilla ice cream
to serve

PREPARATION TIME: approx. 40 minutes (plus baking time)

Pre-heat the oven to 180 °C (Gas Mark 4). Butter a gratin dish. Cut the rinds off the bread rolls, and cut the bread into very small cubes (no more than 0.5 cm long). Place on a baking tray and toast for 10 minutes. Remove from the oven and leave to cool.

Cut the butter into pieces and melt in a saucepan. Mix the sugar, cinnamon and lemon zest in a bowl. Combine the bread cubes with the sugar mixture and half the butter.

Wash, dry, peel and quarter the apples. Cut out the cores and cut the flesh into thin slices. Combine in a bowl with the lemon juice.

Spread one-third of the breadcrumbs over the base of the gratin dish. Arrange half the apples on top. Then spread over another third of the breadcrumbs, and cover with the remainder of the apples. Top with the remainder of the breadcrumbs. Drizzle over teaspoons of the apple juice. Dot with the remainder of the butter to finish.

Bake in the middle of the oven for about 30 minutes until the top is nice and brown. Remove and spoon onto plates. Serve with a dollop of whipped cream and a ball of vanilla ice cream.

NUTRITION INFORMATION: 510 kcal I 2120 kJ I 5 g protein I 22 g fat I 72 g carbohydrate

Pumpkin pie

Makes 12 slices
(1 springform tin, 26 cm diameter)

FOR THE PASTRY
250 g flour
125 g butter
1 egg yolk
20 g sugar
pinch of salt

FOR THE TOPPING
1 small pumpkin (approx. 900 g)
3 eggs
big pinch of salt
175 g brown sugar
200 ml condensed milk
50 g cream cheese
1 tsp cinnamon
big pinch of ground ginger
pinch of nutmeg

ADDITIONALLY
butter for the springform tin

PREPARATION TIME: approx. 40 minutes (plus chilling and baking time)

To make the pastry, sift the flour into a bowl. Add the butter in small pieces, the egg yolk, sugar and salt. Quickly knead together to make a smooth dough. Butter the base and sides of the springform tin. Put the dough in the tin and work evenly over the base with your hands, shaping a small rim up the side. Cover the tin with foil and chill for at least 1 hour.

Pre-heat the oven to 180 °C (Gas Mark 4). Line a baking tray with baking parchment. To make the topping, wash and quarter the pumpkin, then cut into wedges. Peel. Scoop out the seeds and fibres from the inside. Place the wedges on the baking tray and bake for about 40 minutes. The pumpkin should not start to turn brown, so cover with aluminium foil if necessary. Remove and leave to cool, then purée until smooth.

Take the springform out of the refrigerator and remove the foil, then pierce the base several times with a fork. Pre-bake in the middle of the oven for about 8 minutes. Remove from the oven and leave to cool.

Separate the eggs. Whisk the egg whites with the salt until stiff, then add half the sugar. Continue whisking until the mixture is stiff again and the sugar crystals have dissolved. Whisk the egg yolks and the remainder of the sugar until thick and creamy. Add the condensed milk, cream cheese and spices. Whisk until smooth, then gradually whisk in the pumpkin purée. Finally, fold in the whisked egg whites.

Spread the pumpkin mixture over the pastry. Smooth over the surface and bake in the middle of the oven for about 50 minutes. Remove and leave in the tin for a few minutes, then loosen the side of the tin and carefully allow the cake to slide out onto a cake plate. Leave until completely cool.

NUTRITION INFORMATION: 300 kcal | 1250 kJ | 7 g protein | 14 g fat | 37 g carbohydrate

Peach cobbler

Serves 4

500 g ripe peaches
1 tbsp lemon juice
1 tsp grated zest of 1 unwaxed lemon
1 tbsp amaretto
90 g brown sugar
1 tsp cornflour
big pinch of freshly grated ginger
125 g flour
50 g ground almonds
big pinch of baking soda
big pinch of baking powder
pinch of salt
100 g soft butter
1 sachet vanilla sugar
1 egg
50 ml buttermilk

ADDITIONALLY

butter for the dish
icing sugar to dust
whipped cream to serve

PREPARATION TIME: approx. 40 minutes (plus baking time)

Pre-heat the oven to 180 °C (Gas Mark 4). Grease a gratin dish with butter. Cut a cross in the peaches and blanche in boiling water for about 1 minute. Place in a sieve and hold under running cold water. Peel off the skin. Cut the peaches in half and remove the stones. Cut the flesh into wedges.

Combine the wedges in a bowl with the lemon juice and zest, amaretto, 1 tablespoon of sugar, the cornflour and ginger.

To make the sponge, stir together the flour, almonds, baking soda, baking powder and salt. Whisk together the soft butter, the remainder of the sugar and the vanilla sugar until fluffy, then whisk in the egg. Finally, add the buttermilk and whisk until smooth. Pour over with the flour mixture, and stir until smooth.

Put the peach mixture in the dish and spoon the sponge mixture over the top. Bake in the middle of the oven for about 35 minutes until golden. Remove from the oven and dust with icing sugar while still warm. Serve with a dollop of whipped cream.

Tip: You can vary the cobbler by using any seasonal fruit. Cherries are also an excellent choice, for instance, as are apricots. A little grated (white) chocolate is also a very delicious option.

NUTRITION INFORMATION: 560 kcal | 2350 kJ | 10 g protein | 30 g fat | 63 g carbohydrate

Pecan pie

PREPARATION TIME: approx. 25 minutes (plus chilling and baking time)

To make the pastry, cut the butter into small pieces and quickly knead with the remainder of the ingredients. Butter a springform tin, and press the pastry into it with your hands. Make a little rim around the sides. Cover with foil and chill for about 1 hour.

Pre-heat the oven to 180 °C (Gas Mark 4). To make the filling, first melt the butter, and then remove from the hob. Cream together the eggs, egg yolk, sugar and salt until thick and creamy. Pour over the sugar beet syrup, and combine well. Stir in the lukewarm butter, followed by 30 g of ground pecan nuts. Then fold in 150 g of pecan nut halves.

Pierce the pastry base several times with a fork. Arrange the remainder of the ground pecan nuts on top and pour over the filling. Garnish with the remainder of the pecan nut halves. Bake in the middle of the oven for about 50 minutes.

Leave in the springform tin for about 10 minutes, then loosen the side of the tin and carefully allow the pie to slide out onto a cake plate. Serve when quite cold, accompanied by a dollop of cream.

Makes 12 slices
(1 springform tin, 26 cm diameter)

FOR THE PASTRY
100 g butter
200 g flour
50 g ground pecan nuts
50 g sugar
pinch of salt
1 egg

FOR THE TOPPING
100 g butter
4 eggs
1 egg yolk
125 g brown sugar
pinch of salt
150 ml light sugar beet syrup
50 g ground pecan nuts
200 g pecan nut halves

ADDITIONALLY
butter for the springform tin
whipped cream to serve

NUTRITION INFORMATION: 490 kcal | 2060 kJ | 9 g protein | 35 g fat | 37 g carbohydrate

Apple pie

Makes 12 slices
(1 springform tin, 26 cm diameter)

FOR THE PASTRY
200 g butter
350 g flour
50 g sugar
pinch of salt
50 ml cold water

FOR THE FILLING
1 kg tart apples
1 tbsp lemon juice
1 tsp grated zest of 1 unwaxed lemon
175 g brown sugar
2 sachets vanilla sugar
big pinch of cinnamon
1 tbsp cornflour
30 g butter

ADDITIONALLY
butter for the springform tin
flour for the work surface
1 egg yolk and milk to glaze
whipped cream to serve

PREPARATION TIME: approx. 50 minutes (plus chilling and baking time)

To make the pastry, cut the butter into pieces and quickly knead with the remainder of the ingredients. Butter the base and sides of the springform tin and line with two-thirds of the pastry, shaping a 4 cm rim up the side. Cover and chill for about 1 hour. Wrap the remainder of the pastry in foil and chill.

For the apple filling, wash, dry, peel and quarter the apples. Cut out the cores and cut the flesh into slices. Combine in a bowl with the lemon juice. Stir in the lemon zest and both sugars. Sift over the cinnamon and cornflour and fold in.

Pierce the pastry several times with a fork. Arrange the apple mixture on top. Dot flakes of butter over the apples. Fold the protruding edge of the pastry back over the filling. Then roll out the remainder of the pastry out on a worktop and cut into strips about 2 cm wide. Arrange in a grid over the apple filling so only small areas of it are visible through the pastry strips. Press down well on the edges.

Whisk together the egg yolk and a little milk and brush over the surface of the pastry. Bake the pie in the middle of the oven for about 1 hour. Cover loosely with aluminium foil if the surface starts to get too dark.

Leave the pie in the tin for about 15 minutes, then loosen the side of the tin and carefully allow the pie to slide out onto a cake plate. Leave until quite cold, and serve with a little whipped cream. You can also bake and serve the pie in a pie dish.

NUTRITION INFORMATION: 390 kcal I 1620 kJ I 3 g protein I 17 g fat I 55 g carbohydrate

Cinnamon rolls
with cream cheese frosting

Makes 20

FOR THE PASTRY
250 ml milk
50 g butter
500 g flour
pinch of salt
1 sachet dried yeast
2 tbsp sugar
1 egg at room temperature

FOR THE FILLING
125 g butter
100 g pecan nuts (or walnuts)
130 g brown sugar
2 tsp cinnamon

FOR THE FROSTING
40 g butter at room temperature
100 g cream cheese
125 g icing sugar
3–4 drops butter vanilla flavouring

ADDITIONALLY
flour for the work surface

PREPARATION TIME: approx. 30 minutes (plus standing and baking time)

To make the dough, start by warming the milk. Melt the butter in the milk. Remove the saucepan from the hob and leave until the mixture is lukewarm.

Sift the flour into a bowl. Stir in the salt, dried yeast and sugar. Add the egg, and then the milk and butter mixture. Knead together for about 5 minutes until you have a smooth, slightly sticky dough. Cover the bowl with a towel and leave in a warm place for about 1 hour until the dough has doubled in size.

To make the filling, melt 50 g of butter. Chop one half of the nuts and grind the other half. Combine with the sugar, cinnamon and melted butter.

Line a baking tray with baking parchment. Knead the dough well. Roll out to a rectangle on a floured worktop (approx. 40 x 60 cm). Spread the cinnamon mixture over the top, and then roll the dough along the long side. Cut the rolls into slices about 2–3 cm thick and place on the baking tray. Place a tea towel loosely over the tray, and leave to rise for a further 30 minutes. Pre-heat the oven to 180 °C (Gas Mark 4). Melt the remainder of the butter and brush over the cinnamon rolls while lukewarm. Bake in the middle of the oven for about 20 minutes.

To make the frosting, whisk together the butter and cream cheese until smooth. Gradually sift in the icing sugar, whisking all the time. Finish with the butter vanilla flavouring. Spoon the frosting into a piping bag and pipe over the cinnamon rolls. Best served lukewarm, fresh out of the oven.

NUTRITION INFORMATION: 290 kcal | 1210 kJ | 5 g protein | 15 g fat | 33 g carbohydrate

Chocolate doughnuts

PREPARATION TIME: approx. 40 minutes (plus rising time)

Warm the milk and melt the butter in it. Remove from the hob and cool slightly until the mixture is only lukewarm.

Combine the flour, dried yeast, vanilla sugar and salt in a bowl. Stir in the egg and egg yolk. Pour over the milk mixture and 30 ml lukewarm water. Knead together for about 5 minutes until you have a light and airy dough. Note: At this point, it will still be quite sticky. Cover the bowl with a tea towel and leave in a warm place for about 1 hour until the dough has doubled in size.

Line two baking trays with baking parchment. Dust the dough with flour and knead thoroughly. Roll out onto a floured worktop to a thickness of 0.5–1 cm. Cut out dough-nuts, e. g. with a glass of the right diameter. Place the doughnuts on the baking trays, not too close together. Cover loosely with tea towels and leave to rise for about 40 minutes.

Heat the oil for deep-frying to 175 °C. Deep-fry the doughnuts for about 2 minutes on each side. Lift out with a slotted spoon, and place on paper towels to drain.

Heat the chocolate glaze over a hot bain-marie or in the microwave until liquid. Dip one flat side of the doughnuts into the glaze and cover half of them in it. Place on a wire rack to set.

Makes 25

200 ml milk
75 g butter
500 g flour
2 sachets dried yeast
1 sachet vanilla sugar
1 tsp salt
1 egg at room temperature
1 egg yolk
200 g chocolate glaze

ADDITIONALLY
flour for the work surface and to dust
oil for deep-frying

NUTRITION INFORMATION: 170 kcal | 730 kJ | 4 g protein | 8 g fat | 21 g carbohydrate

Recipe index

Picture credits